THE JESUS COMMUNITY

For Ruth Minika Ingesi Ungaya,
a mother to so many

THE JESUS COMMUNITY

Reflections on the Gospel for the B-cycle

Joseph G. Donders

ORBIS BOOKS

Maryknoll, New York 10545

The Catholic Foreign Mission Society of America (Maryknoll) recruits and trains people for overseas missionary service. Through Orbis Books Maryknoll aims to foster the international dialogue that is essential to mission. The books published, however, reflect the opinions of their authors and are not meant to represent the official position of the society.

Library of Congress Cataloging in Publication Data

Donders, Joseph G.
  The Jesus community.

  Includes index.
  1. Church year meditations. I. Title
BX2170.C55D62   1981   242'.3   81-38429
ISBN 0-88344-242-6 (pbk.)   AACR2

Manufactured in the United States of America

CONTENTS

viii   CONTENTS

INTRODUCTION

Mark's gospel
is the oldest report
on Jesus.
It is not
a biography.
It is an account
of how a group of believers
responded to him.
>Mark tried
>to answer the questions
>that lived among
>and around them.
>Why did they believe?
>Why did they come together?
>What did they hope for?
>Why had they developed
>an alternative lifestyle?
Mark answered those queries
by describing
to them
the responses and reactions
of Christ's first followers.
He used those earlier experiences
to clarify
to himself and the others
what had happened to them
when they fell
under the spell
of Jesus.
>We don't know
>where that community
>lived.

Some say in Rome:
"Wasn't Mark the secretary
and interpreter of Peter?"
Some say in Alexandria:
"Isn't Mark considered
to be the founder
of the Christian community
in that African town?"
We in Nairobi,
that other African town,
tried to do together
what Mark did.
We went through
his gospel
in order to understand
what happened to *us;*
in order to see
what *we* saw in Christ;
in order to examine
why *we* felt attracted to him;
in order to analyze
how he "bewitched" *us,*
inviting *us*
to follow
him.

The first thing
Jesus did,
after his call
and his lonely stay
in the desert,
was
—according to Mark—
to ask
Simon and Andrew,
James and John
to be with
him.
He did not want to remain
alone.

He did not want us
to follow him alone
either.
He picked a group
from the road.
He did not select
nor test them.
He took the first ones
he met.
That is what
he did
to all of us,
coming
from all kinds of cultures,
from age-old human groups
Gikuyu and Masai,
Nandi and Idaho,
Kipsigis and Turkana,*
too many to mention
them all.
    Very different
    and yet one
    in our celebration
    and commemoration
    of that one
    who brought us
    TOGETHER
    around his person,
    his bread and his wine:
    his community.
    Why and how
    did he do it?
    What did we see
    in him?
Struggling with those issues
we followed the order
of the liturgical-year cycle B.
That is why twenty-nine
of our reflections are on Mark,

eighteen on the gospel of John,
five on Luke,
and two on Matthew.
     He picked us
     together
     to be with him,
     to change this world,
     to switch over to
     a new style of human life.
The life
we will live
in all time
to come.
Thanks be to
God.

---

* Some of the Kenyan peoples from whom the students in the community hail.

1.

ONLY BEGINNING

Mark 13: 33–37

Every beginning
is difficult,
and very often
the beginning
is the end.
> The beginning
> is difficult:
> you have been postponing
> a task or a study
>> one week,
>> two weeks,
>> six weeks . . .
> and you say:
> "I must start
> today,"
> and you go to your room,
> and you clear your desk,
> and you take your books,
> and you sit down,
> and you take your pencil,
> and you sharpen its point,
> you lick its other end,
> you open your books,
> you look at the date
> on your watch
> and you say:

"After all,
why should I start today?"
and you walk
off.
Very often
the beginning
is the end.
You come together
in a meeting,
criticism is leveled,
programs are made,
a committee appointed,
a chairman elected,
and
—though there is not a penny—
a treasurer too,
a journal is founded,
a club started,
regulations made,
members recruited,
minutes taken down;
everybody is full of enthusiasm
when going home.
But is it not true
that that very often is
all that happens?
The beginning was
the end.
In this advent
we start to prepare
for a new birth
at Christmas.
Every single year
we Christians
prepare for that beginning
again and again,
seemingly admitting
that the beginning last year
was a non-starter,

or even,
maybe,
an end.
　　Some years ago
　　on Christmas
　　I was in a church in Holland,
　　a large church,
　　a church like a factory hall.
　　That church was never
　　full during the year,
　　but that Christmas night
　　it was full,
　　absolutely crammed.
There was a large Christmas scene
next to the altar
at the front of the church,
a life-size stable
with life-size statues
of Joseph and Mary,
the shepherds,
the ox and the donkey,
the sheep,
and in the center of all
the baby in a crib,
just born.
　　The crowd kept growing
　　and the people from the back
　　pushed the people in front
　　into that stable.
　　The faithful
　　stood in between those animals
　　of plaster,
　　and there were so many of them
　　that someone took the crib
　　with the baby,
　　putting it in a corner
　　to protect it
　　from the pressure
　　of the crowd.

After that mass
the parish priest literally glowed
with satisfaction;
he rubbed his hands
and said to us
—with a stealthy look
at the money in the collection bags—
"Happy Christmas,
how good it is to see
that they did not lose
their good old faith."
> The sacristan,
> a wise old man,
> who grew up in that church
> answered:
> "They never have any difficulty
> in celebrating the beginning,
> but that is all they do."
We seem to be quite willing
to accept Jesus
as a baby.
We celebrate his birth
more than any other feast.
We like to see Jesus
as a suckling,
who cannot speak
nor counsel,
a helpless and harmless
little toddler
sucking the breast of his mother
and in no way capable
of challenging our lives.
> But to accept him
> in his adulthood
> at the height of his mission
> telling us to be on our guard,
> to stay awake,
> and to do our duty
> in the building of the kingdom
> to come:

that is something
else.
Some years ago
in a small Christian community
in a West African country,
Upper Volta,
some catechists and church-elders
came together with their priest
in a village called Baam.
They wanted to discuss
something.
It had suddenly struck them
that they spent most of their
pastoral work
on the preparation of the people
who wanted to be baptized
and on the instruction and preparation
of children
for their first confession,
for their first holy communion,
and their confirmation.
    They said:
    "We spend all our time
    on the beginning
    and hardly any time on
       the baptized,
       the adults,
       the core,
       and the kernel
    of our community.
They added:
"True,
Jesus said
that he came to bring fire,
but we made that fire
into a bushfire,
a fire in very, very dry grass,
very fiery
in an ever-growing circle
engaging more and more grass,

but cooling down
in the center where
it started;
cooling down
in that center
and turning into
grey, bitter ashes."
    We
    were in that center
    years ago;
    the fire passed from us
    to others
    ages ago.
    In us,
    very often,
    only ashes and cinders are left.
    The beginning seemed
    to be the end.
Let us pray and hope
that this time
green, very green, new life
may be born in us,
life as fresh
as that baby to be born;
let us pray and hope
that this time
it grows
with us.

2.

IN THE WILDERNESS

Mark 1:1–8

John came out of the
desert
to preach in the
wilderness.
>   Luke is more precise
>   than Mark.
>   Luke describes
>   and situates
>   the wilderness
>   in which John preached
>   exactly:
>>   Tiberius,
>>   a foreign master,
>>   was the emperor;
>>   Pontius Pilate
>>   his colonial representative;
>>   Herod, Philip, and Lysanias
>>   were the local puppets;
>>   and Annas and Caiphas
>>   the spiritual collaborators.
>   It was in that jungle,
>   and under that leadership
>   that the word of God
>   came to John.
>   And he went through
>   the whole of that wilderness
>   to preach:

11

repentance,
forgiveness,
and change.
Repentance *now,*
forgiveness for the *past,*
change for the *future.*
The wilderness
he preached in
was his own country.
A wilderness
not coming
from the hands of God,
but a jungle
caused by innumerable
human decisions
that were
        wrong,
        shortsighted,
        and selfish.
Decisions
that had created havoc
in the lives
of the many.
        It was in that
        jungle
        that John preached
        and baptized.
As long
as we think
about John
like that
—preaching
in his own country
two thousand years ago—
his preaching
remains distant
and very far
away.

Let us try
to get that wilderness
and also John's word
nearer home,
so that it can cut us
to the bone.
Let us speak
about the wilderness
in which we live.
And let us think
not only of sin
but of the world
we are accustomed
to.
Yesterday
I asked over there
in the sacristy
a small boy
who came for some candles:
"What is your name?"
He said something
I didn't understand.
So I asked:
"What did you say?"
And he said:
"Number six."
I said:
"Number six?"
"Yes,"
he answered,
"out of forty-one."
I had asked
his name.
He gave me his
ranking
in class!
He indicated
at the same time

one of those things
that make education and schooling
in this country
and in this world
so terribly
wrong.
        That schooling
        breeds strife;
        it has war
        built in;
        it is based on
        pushing and pulling,
        getting first over
        the heads and bodies
        of others.
We wonder
about the actual violence
among students
in and outside school,
after having forced them
to be violent
all the time:
a human-made
blackboard jungle.
        A boy,
        Samson Mwangi,
        thirteen years old,
        made together with another
        250,000 boys and girls
        his *final* primary-school examination
        some weeks ago.
        When he was at question 31
        —out of ninety multiple-choice questions—
        he suddenly drew a blank;
        he did not see anything
        anymore;
        the strain of the exam
        and the preparation for it,
        had become too much.

He put up his hand
through the fog in which
he suddenly lived.
Under *supervision*
of a fully grown adult
supervisor
he was allowed to leave the room;
under supervision
he was allowed to wash his face;
and under supervision
he was escorted
back to the examination room.
Primary school, thirteen years old,
and the lesson is
no one can be trusted
at all.
The wilderness
in which we try
to live.
Oh, brother, oh, sister,
so many more examples
could be given
about this
man-eat-man forest
in which we
wither.
It is in that forest,
in that jungle
that the word of God
sounds
through John,
saying that once
justice and integrity
are victorious,
the whole of humankind
will be saved,
that Jesus, the savior,
is going to bring
a total difference.

But indicating also
where we come in and
what we should do:
    straightening the paths
    we are walking now,
    preparing a way for the Lord,
    filling the valleys and potholes,
    leveling the mountains and obstacles
    in us
    and in the lives
    we live.
If we all do
that,
his coming
will be smooth
and peaceful.
One example will do:
it is the story
of a student at this university.
All had been stolen
from him.
He borrowed some money
and went to town
to buy something
to dress with.
He chose a pair of pants
for 169 Kenyan shillings.
When he went to get
his cheety*
to pay,
the cashier,
obviously not the owner
of the shop,
whispered to him:
"If you give forty shillings
to me,
I will write only
one-hundred-and-nineteen,
and the rest is for you."

The temptation
was great,
the crooked, winding road
wide open
to him.
But he said:
"No, write
one-hundred-and-sixty-nine;
I am a Christian."
It is only like
this
that we can prepare
for the efficient coming of Christ
among us.
Not as individuals
but from within
the communities
we form.
Come, Lord Jesus,
come!

*Cash-slip.

3.

THE STRAIGHTNESS OF JOHN

John 1:6–8, 19–28

Suddenly
there was that strange man,
John.
Nobody knew where he came from.
He came from the desert,
but what does that mean?
In the desert
there are no streets,
no villages,
no addresses,
no postbox numbers
and no postoffice.
Where did he come from?
        You could not place him
        either
        by looking for the label
        in his jacket
        to see where he had
        bought it.
        His clothing was not bought,
        it was found;
        it was a camelskin
        tailored
        by God.

He did not even eat
as we eat,
or as they ate:
things mixed, cooked,
stewed, and broiled.
He only ate
the things
as made
by God.
     That seems to have been
     the thing
     about John.
     He was straight.
     He came directly
     out of the hand of God,
     unexpectedly,
     no middle-man,
     from nowhere,
     totally independent,
     untouchable and untouched,
     a mouthpiece only,
     a voice,
     a message
     in the wilderness
     of this old,
     broken world.
No wonder
that they came
from all over the country
to have a look
at this strange man.
No wonder
that their main questions were:
who are you?
where do you come from?
are you a prophet?
do you come from on high?
are you one of our ancestors?

His answer was
a simple one:
"I am a voice,
a voice that cries
in your wilderness,
make straight the way
for the Lord."
And that,
sister and brother,
is quite something!
The hour has
come!
We should be
ready!
The invasion is
near!
John's message is
that we should let ourselves
be invaded
by the Lord
unconditionally:
remove
barriers and obstructions;
fill
waterpuddles and potholes;
straighten
diversions and roundabouts,
bends and angles.
Construct
one
straight road
so that he can crash
in upon us
at full force,
in one go,
with power,
fire,
and might.

We know that things
have to change.
We know that we should
have done more.
We know that even
if we did all we could,
we did not do all
we should have done.

It is in that frustration
and in all frustrations;
it is in that powerlessness,
and in all powerlessnesses,
it is in that wilderness
and in all human jungles
that John,
the prophet,
enters
from the desert
singing
the new song.

A voice of God,
asking us
to give way
to God
in our lives
straight away,
and all will be
good
because all will be
the Lord's.

That is all
he said
and had to say,
the rest would come
with
Him.

4.

THE WILLINGNESS OF MARY

Luke 1:26–38

The melodies of our Christmas songs
are very nice.
We know them all.
But when you look at their words,
theological
and all sorts of other religious
considerations
might make your flesh creep.
> Most of those hymns
> were written a hundred
> or more
> years ago,
> and it is
> as if
> in those times
> Jesus and his coming
> were things
> out of this world.
> Those carols
> sing about angels
> and there is nothing against angels,
> but they definitely
> draw the attention
> away from this earth.

22

They sing about light,
and there is nothing against light,
but the light they sing about
comes from stars,
and stars are high up
and far away
    from this world.
They sing about grace
about peace of soul
about heaven
and its choirs
and it is
as if all that happened
played exclusively
in a world
that has nothing to
with this world,
the world
in which we
        live and breath
        and move.
It is here
that we should be helped
and saved.
        But neither the music
        nor the heavenly fireworks
        deceived Mary,
        when that angel,
        a finger of burning light,
        pointed at her,
        intruding into her life,
        almost ordering her:
            be glad and fear not,
            listen and conceive,
            bear a son and give him a name,
            the name Jesus,
            that means savior
            for all time to come.

She understood
that she was going to be
a cooperator,
the final one
in that long line of women
who had wished
so dearly
and so effectively
to participate
in a new world
to be born.
    Matthew mentions
    four of them
    in his genealogy of
    Jesus.
Tamar,
who feared to be left out,
and who sat
disguised as a prostitute
along the road
to conceive from
Judah.
    Rahab,
    the whore
    in Jericho,
    who felt that God
    was with the Jewish spies
    she had been hiding
    in her house
    and who wanted to be
    in their line
    through her womb.
Ruth,
the stranger,
who sleeping with Boaz
gave birth to Obed,
the grandfather of
David.

Bathsheba,
who bathed herself
—was it to be seen?—
entering like that
into David's line
and the future
to come.
Mary
was going to be
at the end
of that line
of those who according to
orthodox morality
submitted,
in a definitely
rather unorthodox way
to the redeeming plan
of God.
     Mary knew,
     she understood,
     and she said
     without hesitation:
     "Here I am,
     do what you want!"
God interfered in her life
not only by casting
some heavenly light
on her face.
God interfered in her life
not only by sending
a sweet-looking angel
to her.
God interfered in her life
not only by changing her mind
into heavenly peace and bliss;
     God took her
     in her world,
     in her house,

in her life,
in her body,
in her womb,
in all that counts
    and that is how
    he wants to take
    all of us
    at Christmas
    in view of our hopes,
    in view of his promise
    to this world
    and to
    humankind.

5.

A DONKEY THAT RETURNED

Luke 2:1–14

Happy Christmas.
It is midnight;
it could not be earlier
in the morning
of this new day.
    The child is born,
    washed,
    swaddled in some cloths,
    and put in a manger.
That manger
is something special;
it is mentioned
three times
in the report from Luke.
    They laid him
    in a *manger*
    because there was no room
    for them
    in the inn.
The angels
sang to the shepherds:
look for a *manger*.
    It was in a *manger*
    that they found
    him.

27

In every Christmas crib
you find next to Jesus
Mary, of course,
and Joseph too.
But if the crib
is complete
there are also,
next to him in *their manger*,
an ox and
an ass.

> They are not there
> just for decorative purposes;
> they are not there
> just for sentimental reasons;
> they are not there
> because of one or another
> medieval imagination only.

They are there
because of a text
in an old prophetic book,
the one about Isaiah,
who speaking in the name of God
said to his people:

> "The ox knows its owner,
> and the ass its master's manger,
> but you,
> O people of mine,
> you don't know your Lord
> and God" (Isa. 1:3).

An ox knows
where it gets
its sustenance;
an ass knows
where it gets
its food;
but you,
O humanity,
you forgot.

That is how
that manger is a
sign.
That is why
that manger was the place
those shepherds,
representing humanity,
had to go to,
like a donkey
that went astray
and came
home.
They laid him
in a manger
because there was no place
for him
in the inn.
We think
that he was laid
in that crib
because they refused
him
in the inn.
The truth
might be exactly
the opposite.
It was our Lord and God
who refused to stay
in an inn.
He was fed up
with living in hotels and motels,
in inns, pubs, and lodging-houses
in a world
that is really
God's.
Read the prophet Jeremiah
and you will understand.
Jeremiah,

in the name of God,
complained
that whenever God
visited this world,
people did not know about God
any more,
they did not recognize Yahweh,
they closed their doors to God,
they said:
We don't know who you are,
get out.
    And God felt like
    a stranger in this world
    and stopped knocking at the doors
    of those people
    and decided to stay
    like a foreigner
    in an inn (Jer. 14:8-9).
When God
returned to this world
in Jesus
so very long ago,
    he was born in
    a manger.
    And that donkey
    called humankind
    returned to him
    that very night.
It was in that crib
surrounded by Mary, Joseph,
and the shepherds,
that he found a home
again
with us.
    An inn was not necessary
    any more.
    The inn was
    no place
    for him.

In the circle
around that crib
a first,
new human homestead
had been formed
in the light
of angels
and stars.
    The new pattern
    had been
    set.
    The new community
    was born.

6.

MARY HIS MOTHER

Luke 2: 22–40

Luke calls Mary
his mother.
That is a very simple,
and a very nice
title.
It is a true one
too.
    Within the church
    Mary got all kinds of other titles
    like empress
    and queen.
    Titles that don't call up
    her family-role.
    Titles that call up
    rather aloof
    and unrealistic personalities,
    expensively dressed,
    with diamonds and rubies,
    with rustling silk all over,
    with crowns and scepters,
    with hosts of servants,
    and never time
    for anyone.
That is what church leaders,
the careermen,
the rulers,
the his holinesses,
and his excellencies,

and his eminencies
made her:
a ruling queen.
        That is what they hoped her
        to be
        in order
        to rationalize
        and justify
        their interpretation
        of their own position.
But she was
only and simply
the mother of Jesus
the mother of God.
        It is important
        to understand this very well
        so that we do not misunderstand
        God,
        God's work,
        and God's tactics.
If Mary had lived
here and now
then she would not have lived
in Muthaiga,
in Karen,
or in Loresho,*
except, maybe,
in one of the servant's quarters
over there.
        We would have to look for her,
        in Mathare,
        in Kawangware,
        or in Rongai.**
She did not belong
to those people
who were well off
in this world.
She belonged to the poor,
to the lowly
and the common ones.

She knew that very well,
she herself said so.
When she met her aunt Elizabeth
and when Elizabeth greeted her
as mother of the Lord,
she suddenly burst out
in a song,
which must have been hidden
in her head and her heart
since she had conceived.
She exploded
so to speak
and sang:
"My soul shout out,
and my spirit rejoice
because God
looked upon his lowly handmaid,
the almighty did great things to me.
The rich he overlooked,
the poor he filled with glory,
thanks to his powerful arm."
She shouted out for joy,
because God
bends over
those in need.
There is a kind of logic
in all this.
A logic we can all understand
if we want to.
It is the logic
of the Old Testament,
it is the logic
of the New Testament:
God created life,
God is interested
in the life
God created.
God is interested
in that life
when it flourishes,

but God is also interested
in that life
when it withers,
is frustrated,
>   thwarted,
>   handicapped,
>   or diminished.
It is to that handicapped,
that diminished life
that God's helping hands
reach out first,
just like our own hands
reach out first to
those parts of our body
that ache.
>   That is what Mary
>   understood
>   and that is why she jumped
>   with joy.
>   That is what we should
>   understand,
>   knowing that there is
>   hope,
>   that God doesn't leave
>   this world
>   alone,
>   that peace will come,
>   that pain will be taken away,
>   if we accept
>   God's hands,
>   God's life-giving power and might
>   as Mary did.
>   Mary:
>   the mother of God
>   in this world,
>   the mother of God
>   in us.

*Rich residential areas of Nairobi.
**Slum areas in Nairobi.

7.

THEY FOLLOWED A STAR

Matthew 2: 1–12

When the star appeared
those three wise men
must have been living
a certain type of life.
  They were teachers or kings,
  philosophers or sages,
  nobody really knows,
  but one thing we do know,
  when they saw the star
  they decided
  to stop their routine
  and to risk
  something
  new.
They climbed
over the edge
of their existence
and they followed
that star.
  We might think
  that that was easy
  for them.
  It was not easy
  at all.
  All through human history
  there are stories and reports
  on how difficult it is
  to change.

When in the enormously popular
bestseller:
Jonathan Livingston Seagull
Jonathan explains
to the other seagulls,
that seagulls
can live a much higher,
                        fuller,
                        wider
                        and further life
than they do,
the others did not want
to believe him,
and when he showed them
that it was really possible,
they threw him out of their circle
and banned him.
        But do we really need
        that story
        to know
        how difficult a change
        really is?
Even the most common changes
in our lives
are difficult:
        To repair a leaking tap,
        to start a more efficient bookkeeping,
        to re-arrange a room,
        to clean a cupboard,
        to go to the doctor,
        to write a letter,
        to come to a reconciliation
        and shake a hand,
it is often not done;
though the light appeared,
the idea flashed,
the star shone,
it was not followed,
nothing happened.
All remained the same.

Those three men
were wise,
because when they saw
that new star
indicating
    a new life,
    a new king,
    a new ruler,
    a new child
    they followed faithfully
    notwithstanding
    all the risks.
Let us follow it
too
until
we arrive.
    Some time ago
    I met a priest
    who had been working
    for forty-five years
    in this country,
    following that star
    faithfully
    all those years.
    He asked me
    very sincerely:
    "What was the use
    of all that I did?
    Did things really improve,
    did we come any nearer to God,
    what did it help?"
He forgot
at that moment of depression,
that a baby was born,
that a seed had been sowed,
that a growth process
had been started,
an evolution
and not a revolution.

God could have given
the tree,
but God did give
the seed.
God could have made us as
already processed saints,
but God did want us
to grow.
God could have flown
those three wise men
over to Bethlehem
by angelic air express,
but God gave them
that star,
which they followed
slowly
but surely,
until they arrived
where the star
stopped
to find what they had been
looking for:
    a new child,
    a new rule,
    a new king,
    a new life.

8.

THE HOME-LIFE TEST

John 1:35–42

John and Andrew
were the first ones
who started to follow
him,
first almost on the sly
and very shy,
but slowly from
nearer and nearer,
until he noticed
them.
He stopped,
turned around,
and said:
      "You are following me,
      what do you want?"
They said:
      "Where do you
      live?"
He said:
      "Come and see,
      you are welcome."
          And they went
          with him
          to his home,
          the house where he lodged.
          They stayed with him,

40

and it is during their stay
at his home
that they started
to believe in him,
so much so
that the very next day,
they told others:
"We found the Messiah,
the person sent to save us."
They discovered
this
at his home,
from the way
in which he acted,
        reacted and
        interacted *there*.
During the meeting of the
World Council of Churches
some years ago
over here in Nairobi,
a famous liberation-theologian
had come from overseas.
He spoke in this very chapel
        about oppression,
        liberation,
        about social and other
        justice.
He spoke about:
"God-is-with-the-poor";
and about
"God-is-not-with-the-rich."
        At that point a listener
        stood up
        and said:
        "I hear that you are
        very rich,
        that you own three houses,
        for each season one.

You spoke very nice,
indeed,
but what about your own life,
what about your home,
which side are you on?"
Those remarks did not do away
with the force of the arguments
of the speaker,
but they did away
with his personal credibility.
He in his life,
in the way he acted,
      reacted, and
      interacted
was not going to be of any help
in this world.

     About a year ago
     a bishop
     came to address
     the students over here
     on this campus.
     His topic was:
     The role of the Christian
     in politics."
     He developed a whole plan
     on how to build a
     just society
     according to the spirit
     of Jesus Christ.
In question-time
a student stood up
and asked
why the bishop
owned so many houses,
among others the one
that student's family lived in,
and why he had increased
the rents of his tenants
so pitilessly.

There was no
answer.
    The student's remarks
    did not invalidate
    the arguments
    of that bishop.
    But that bishop,
    too,
    could not be taken
    as an example
    of how to help this world
    to become a better,
    a more human and a more divine
    place.
Their home-lives
betrayed them.
    In the case of Jesus
    his home-life
    did not betray
    his words.
It was precisely
his home-life
that made John and Andrew
say:
"He is the
savior."
    Sister or brother,
    John and Andrew
    taught us
    how we can test
    others,
    but they taught us
    also
    how we can test
    ourselves,
    the sincerity of our
    intentions,
    the honesty of our
    being.

It is
in the way
we treat others
at home
that we prove
our faith in
him.

9.

HE CALLED THEM AT ONCE

Mark 1: 14–20

John's task had been,
relatively,
easy.
He had to announce
the end.
He drew
the curtain.
He was
the full-stop.
He wound up
all that had ever been
before,
the good and
the bad.
> John had gone
> into the desert
> to contemplate
> the end;
> he came out
> with
> a funeral lament:
> "The axe is at the roots,
> the tree of life is going
> to fall!"
> Jesus had gone
> into the desert
> to meditate on
> the beginning;

45

he came out
with
an entrance hymn:
"The time has come,
the kingdom is close
at hand."
John preached
but stayed
alone.
In the end
everyone is
alone.
Jesus preached,
but he could not
and he would not
stay alone.

     John stepped out of
     this world
     with its pattern
     of human intrigue
     and hurting sin.
     Jesus stepped into
     this world
     with its pattern
     of divine promise
     and life to come.
That *"stepping-in"*
was the first thing
he did,
before any miracle
at all.
The greatest sign of
what
he wanted to bring.

     He called
     just from alongside his road,
     the first ones
     he found:
     Simon and Andrew,
     James and John.

He did not
select them.
He just happened
to meet them,
a random sample
of all those
to come.
    He took them away
    from the ways of a world
    that was doomed
    into the new community
    to come,
    with the immediate promise
    to them
    that they too
    would not stay
    alone:
    "I will make you fishers
    of men."
A net full of fish,
a tree full of fruits,
a field with pearls,
a sheepfold full,
    with guests around a table,
    and bread really shared,
    with wine going round,
    and God's family built,
        with Peter as
        a guide,
        with Andrew
        querying,
        with James
        for the practical things,
        with John
        for his vision
           and with HIM
           at the head
           of that
           life-giving
           table.

10.

AN OBJECT LESSON

Mark 1: 21–28

They waited
until the sabbath
and went that day
with him
to the synagogue.
>   He spoke,
>   he taught,
>   everyone was impressed
>   and amazed.
>   They looked at each other
>   and said:
>   "Where did he get it,
>   unbelievable,
>   and so self-confident,
>   such an authority!"
Simon was the one
who told Mark,
>   —according to some his son
>   and according to others his clerk—
but he does not seem
to have remembered
what Jesus said that day.
>   Most probably
>   Jesus talked in the way
>   anyone talks
>   who wants to change the
>   human situation.

48

He must have given
an analysis,
he must have been drawing
conclusions,
he must have been suggesting
some recommendations:
words, words, words.
Simon had no interest
in those words at all.
He passed them over.
His interest was
in something else;
he was interested
in what Jesus did.
    There was, he reported,
    a man in that synagogue
    possessed by an evil spirit.
    That evil spirit
    talked too.
    It shouted:
    "Do you want to destroy us,
    do you really want *to do*
    something about us?
    I know who you are,
    the Holy One of God."
And Jesus told
that spirit
to be quiet
and to get out,
and that evil spirit
got quiet
and wriggled itself
out of that man,
who with a loud cry
was liberated
and free
there and then.
    It was at Puebla,
    ten years after Medellín,

that the Latin American cardinals
and bishops
met again.
One of them,
Dom Helder Camara,
said:
"Medellín
produced beautiful statements,
an excellent analysis,
and very good recommendations,
but,"
he added,
"nothing really
happened.
The church is still
with the rich,
in order to be able to help
the poor
who are poor
because of those rich!"
No evil spirit
had been chased away;
after all those words
everything had remained
the same or worse
than ever before.
When Mark wrote
his Gospel,
he was not interested
in what Jesus said
or taught;
there are hardly any
references
to anything of the kind.
He was more interested
in what Jesus did.
He chased an evil spirit
away,

as a demonstration,
an object lesson
showing
what he had come
to do.
We his disciples
should *do*
the same.
We should,
through our studies and words,
locate evil,
but once that is done,
let us not repeat and repeat;
let us chase
evil
out.

11.

SO THAT I CAN PREACH

Mark 1: 29–39

The report is about
Jesus' first full
working-day.
  He had preached
  in the synagogue.
  He had chased away
  his first evil spirit.
  He had healed
  Peter's mother-in-law.
  The rumor had spread
  during that sabbathday,
  while nobody was allowed
  to move.
But at sunset,
once the sabbath was over,
they started to come
from all sides
with their sick
and bedevilled ones.
The whole town
came crowding
at the door.
  He healed quite
  a number of them,
  but he could not heal
  them all.
  He simply did not
  have the time.

From that very first day
they had manuevered him
into an impossible
situation.
> Just imagine
> opening a hospital
> for all the sick,
> free of charge.
> Impossible,
> especially if healing
> is guaranteed,
> instantaneous
> and everlasting.
Think of the queues,
the pushing and the pulling,
the sanitation problems,
and the police you would need
to keep some
order.
> That night
> he went to bed
> very tired.
> I think
> that he didn't sleep
> at all.
> Early in the morning
> he heard the first
> sick ones
> come again.
> He got up,
> he slipped through
> the back door
> out of the house
> to a lonely place
> to pray.
But when the queue
had formed itself
at full length,
his disciples went out
to fetch him.

Simon took the
lead.
They found him
and they said:
"Come,
everybody is waiting
for you."
He refused,
he did not come.
He knew that he could not
do it
alone.
He knew
that even his shoulders
were neither broad nor strong
enough
to carry all sickness
and suffering
in that way.
He knew
that he had not come
to start a health enclave,
a kind of Lourdes
before its
time.

> He had come
> to heal,
> but he could not do it
> alone,
> and that is why
> he answered,
> that he preferred
> to preach
> to get the others,
> to get us
> involved.

It was his first conflict
with Simon,
later called by him Peter.

It was his first conflict
with his community
that wanted *him*
to perform,
to carry the load,
while they would look on
and direct the queue,
remaining,
they themselves,
the same.
> They did not understand
> what he had said
> in the synagogue
> of Nazareth,
> that he had come
> to heal
> *"the broken-hearted!"*
> He wanted to heal
> Simon and Andrew,
> James and John,
> and you and me
> in that brokenness
> of our hearts
> that does not let us
> move
> while the poor are hungry,
> and our old parents lonely,
> while babies are dying
> and children are lost,
> while wars are waged
> and irreplaceable minerals wasted,
> while the trees
> and animals are exterminated,
> while useless things are advertised,
> and young virgins sold.
They said:
"Stay here
and heal,
be good."

He said:
"No,
I have to go
to preach
and heal
where you
yourself
need
to be healed."
And he
went.

12.

DON'T TELL ANYONE

Mark 1:40–45

A leper came to
him.
He fell on his knees
in front of him
and he pleaded
with his right hand
over his mouth:
"If you want to,
you can heal me."
      Jesus looked at him,
      that creature of his,
      his brother,
      and once again
      he was touched with pity
      and he said:
      "Of course
      I want to:
      be healed!"
But having learned
from what had happened
to him before,
he added:
      "But, please,
      don't tell anyone,
      except the priests
      you need
      to get your
      health-certificate."

The man did not go only
to those priests;
he told
his story
left, right,
and center
and there they came again,
the hundreds
and the thousands
looking for the easy thing
—his touch—
to be healed
while remaining
unchanged.
       Healed like that leper
       externally
       at the surface
       of his skin.
Like those patients
doctors speak about,
who are looking
for an injection,
an ointment,
a powder,
or a pill,
but who are not willing
to change
their eating habits,
their smoking,
their lifestyle,
or pace.
       Like those sufferers
       from VD
       who are quite ready
       to undergo
       all kinds of treatment
       but who are not prepared
       to stop
       their promiscuity.

Like all those of us
who are willing to discuss
and discuss
all the ills of society and
        how they should be overcome:
        how the goods should be redivided,
        how the poor should be helped,
        how the drunkards should be healed,
        how the prostitutes should be saved,
        how the orphans should be fed,
        how the wars should be stopped
in meeting after meeting after meeting,
minuting all that
carefully
in writing.
        But nothing
        ever happens
        because all
        that happens
        does not go deeper
        than our skins.
Jesus said:
"I will heal
your skin,
I will heal the surface,
but don't tell anyone;
keep it
a secret,
because it is not all,
and if you tell
they will never
understand
what I really came for."
        But the ex-leper
        did tell,
        he was really not changed,
        and Jesus was proved right:
        they came,
        we came,

and we come,
looking for
that easy thing
—his touch—
while remaining
unchanged.

13.

DOUBLE VISION

Mark 2:1–12

The first thing he heard
was that noise on the roof;
the first thing he saw:
the hole in the ceiling;
the first thing he smelled
and tasted:
that cloud of dust.
>   Slowly they lowered
>   their crippled,
>   bedridden friend
>   in front of his feet,
>   anxiously watching
>   his face,
>   because he was preaching
>   that day
>   and not healing.
But that is not all
he saw;
he also saw
their faith,
and because of their faith
he said to their friend:
"Your sins
are forgiven."
>   A great silence
>   fell.
>   Some were disappointed,

they had hoped for a healing:
a man jumping
—with an alleluia—
from his bed.
Others were outraged:
he had gone too far;
he could not do
what he did:
forgive
someone's sins.
He heard their silence,
but that is not all
he heard.
He also heard
their thoughts
in that hush.
       So he said
       to them
       while addressing
       the man
       still on his bed:
       "To show you
       that I forgave you
       your sins,
       take now your bed
       and walk."
That is what he did
and they saw him
walking out;
but that is not all:
they also saw
his sins
forgiven.
       It seems that all those involved
       in the story of today
       had two sources of information.
       Information about what they
       saw with their eyes
       and did not see with their eyes;

information about what they
heard with their ears
and did not hear with their ears;
information about what they
smelled with their noses
and did not smell with their noses;
information about what they
touched with their hands
and did not touch with their hands;
information about what they
tasted in their mouths
and did not taste in their mouths.
That double-up
can be explained
in all kinds
of ways:
we can say that the heart has reasons
the head has not;
we can say that we have rational knowledge
next to an intuitive one;
we can say that we know about the here and now
and about a world to come;
we can say it in very many
different ways.
  We even would be able
  to point out,
  strictly physiologically,
  that modern science
  seems to have proved
  that the two brainlobes
  in our head
  are the interconnected sources
  of those two types of information;
  one reasons and argues,
  the other one listens and intuits,
  and so on,
    but all this naming
    is not so very important.
    Important is this:

if we want to be
a real human being,
if we want to be
like HIM,
then
we
too
need double vision.
I saw at the door
of the chapel today
that there is going to be
a meeting of the
University Young Christian Students.
That UYCS works
according to a method.
Their method seems simple.
It is
     SEE,
     JUDGE,
     ACT.
What is meant
by that
SEE?
     Jesus *saw*
     those men lowering
     their friend
     on his bed
     and
     he *saw*
     their faith.
     Jesus *saw*
     the man
     who was crippled
     and
     he *saw*
     that man's desire
     to be forgiven.
His vision
was double.

The first seeing
is different
from the second one.
That second vision
was about faith,
about sin,
and about God;
they are the things
we meet
in prayer.
>   Are we not too often,
>   all of us,
>   thinking that
>   that first seeing
>   alone
>   can help
>   us
>   in this world?
Are we willing
to *see*
our human situation
in the light
of faith,
sin, and God?
Do we really
have his double sight?
Do we really pray
in the world
in which we live,
>   or do we split
>   our lives:
>   being logical
>   *here*
>   and pious
>   *there*?

14.

WE ARE THE BRIDE

Mark 2:18–22

The occasion
was simple.
Some people came
to him
and said:
    "The followers of John
    and the disciples of the Pharisees
    do fast,
    but your friends
    don't.
    Why not?"
In his answer
—not simple at all—
Jesus
compared himself
to a bridegroom
preparing for marriage
and those friends of his
to his marriage attendants.
He said:
    "I, Jesus,
    am going to take you,
    humankind,
    as my bride.
    My disciples will be
    my witnesses in this;

they cannot very well
fast
preparing
that feast."
All this
might seem
very strange
to us.
Maybe, it did not sound
so strange
to the Hebrews,
because they must have known
from their biblical tradition
that theme
from the prophet
Hosea:
    "Thus says the Lord:
    I am going to get her
    —meaning humankind—
    I will bring her out
    into the wilderness,
    to a very lonely place,
    I will talk to her,
    I will praise her,
    I will tempt her,
    and everything
    will be
    all right."
For us,
it is very difficult
to understand that theme.
It is so mystical,
so very romantic,
so deep,
so very poetical,
and so daring.
It almost embarrasses
us.

One thing
seems obvious.
Jesus did not see
this world
and humanity
in it,
as most of us
do.
For most of us
this world
in which we live
is all there
is.
Whatever you are studying
here at the University,
it is always
this world,
in Arts and Architecture,
in Commerce and Law,
in Engineering and Medicine,
in Agriculture and Science,
in Veterinary Medicine, and even in
Journalism.
We analyze,
measure,
describe,
plan,
and develop
it.
And doing all this
we have been
so successful
that we modern people
got more and more
involved in that world,
up to the point
that we became
almost one-dimensional:

     believing our eyes,
     believing our ears,
     believing our noses,
     believing our fingers,
     believing our tongues
     only.
And even if we
pray,
we think of this world
only:
     we want to be healed
     here;
     we want to be successful
     here;
     we want to live
     as long as possible
     here.
Just as in the time
Jesus lived:
     stop my bleeding,
     and let me have children,
     whispered a woman;
       heal my son,
       he gets convulsions,
       said a father;
     take my skin disease away,
     said the leper;
       bring your friend Lazarus
       back to *this* life,
       asked his sisters.
It was and is
always
about this life.
It is so much
about this life
and this world
that very many Christians
think, or better, believe,

that the resurrection
will mean,
that we,
after our death,
are going to live on
as we are living now
forever
and ever.

      They forget that Jesus
      did not rise
      from the dead
      like Lazarus,
      or that boy in Naim,
      or that other girl,
      but that he rose
      to a different,
      a glorified,
      life.

Would you like
to continue to live
as you are living now
for always?

      Didn't the old African
      call his children
      one day
      to tell them
      that he felt
      that his end in this world
      had come,
      and that he had decided
      to heed death's call?

There is a story
about a monastery
in Brittany
about 1200 years ago.

      In that convent
      nobody died.
      All the monks
      remained living,

and they were very upset
about that.
They got older
and older;
there was no end
in sight.
They decided
to pray
to be allowed
to die.
The prayer was not
heard.
They lived
on and on.
Until the Abbot
had a dream
and in that dream
he noticed
that the gate of heaven
through which
the angels went
up and down,
from and to this world,
was exactly above
their convent.
      Those descending
      and ascending angels
      used the convent-compound
      as their landing-strip
      on earth.
And it was
in that way
that the convent
of those monks
was a kind of illegal extension
of the heavenly court
and that was why
the monks
did not die.

Next morning
he told his story
—after matins—
to the other monks.
And they decided,
there and then,
to break down
their monastery.
That is what
they did.
They shifted it
to another place
a few hundred yards
beyond,
and immediately
they started to die,
the oldest ones first
and they were
very, very happy.

We should not be bound
to the here,
we should not be limited
to the now.
Our possibilities
extend wider
into a kingdom
to come:
a marriage
to be
celebrated
by us
and
by HIM.

15.

PROTESTING AGAINST OURSELVES

Mark 1:12–15

Some days ago Lent began.
Some days ago hundreds of you
marched through the streets of Nairobi
demanding a just and
a better world.
> There should be
> a connection
> between those two.
Last Wednesday was Ash Wednesday
and this chapel was full
with students and staff
who received on their foreheads
the ashes
burnt from the tree branches
that had been used last year
at Palm Sunday
during another demonstration
to hail Christ
as our savior and king.
> By receiving those ashes
> we testified
> in public
> that we are willing
> to commemorate
> the suffering of Jesus Christ
> for forty days,

73

the number of days
he was in the desert.
We are going
to participate
in Jesus' passion.
Very many Christians
take that word
and that idea
of his suffering
in such a way
      that they start to mortify
      themselves;
      that they start to pray
      in a painful position;
      that they start to discipline
      themselves;
      that for forty days they neither eat
      nor drink
      what they would have liked to eat
      and drink.
I wonder
whether that is what Jesus did.
His suffering
was not done
for the sake of suffering.
He did not like to be beaten
      —he would have been abnormal:
      a masochist—
he did not like to be pushed and pulled
through the streets of Jerusalem
      —he would have been abnormal:
      a kind of exhibitionist—
he did not like to die
on the cross.
      He suffered
      with a purpose,
      he suffered
      because that suffering
      was unavoidable,

he suffered
because he wanted
to combat evil and injustice,
sin, and unfaithfulness
in this,
our world.
That is why
he suffered.
His suffering was
that fight.
He was fighting the powers
that had become
so strong in our lands
that they ruled them,
and arrested and
killed
him.

It is in the line
of that fight
that so many of you
demonstrated
in the streets
of Nairobi
for justice
and for
the overthrow
of all evil
that is still
a threat to us
all.
It is in that way
that so many of you
joined his fight
against
all that tries
to suffocate
us.

All this is excellent
and very good,

it is true
and honorable,
it is heroic
and praiseworthy,
　　but we should not be
　　mystified
　　because of all this
　　when we are trying to find out
　　where evil
　　lurks
　　in this society.
　　It hides
　　also
　　in us.
It did *not* hide
in Jesus.
We read today
how,
after his forty days in the desert
the evil in this world came to tempt him:
　　Use your power
　　(and their hunger)
　　to make bread
　　and get rich!
　　　He refused.
　　Use your power
　　(and their credulity)
　　to work a miracle
　　and get honored!
　　　He refused.
　　Use your power
　　(and their need for a leader)
　　to rule
　　over others!
　　　He refused.
When he started
his fight against
the falsehood of his exploiters,

he had
clean hands,
he had
a clean heart,
he had
a clean mind.
    And from that
    most important
    point of view
    he was different
    from us.
    He had no guilt.
    When he asked
    during his trial:
    "What wrong
    did I do?,"
    they had no answer,
    they used
    fake evidence.
When he marched
through the streets
of Jerusalem
protesting
against the powers
and the evils
of his time,
he was not marching
against anything
in himself,
    and that,
    dear sister, dear brother,
    is the difference
    between him
    and me,
    between you
    and him.
The branches you carried
and waved,

were carried and waved
protesting against yourself
also.
     The branches they carried
     and waved around Jesus
     were not carried and waved
     against anything
     in him,
     but definitely
     against something
     in all of us.
And that is
why
we used
the bitterness
of their ashes
against us,
to show on our heads
that we
are guilty
too.

16.

HUMAN GLORY TO COME

Mark 9:2–10

He had come
to struggle
with evil,
but not to suffer
fruitless pain.
    He had come
    to undo the older
    animal powers,
    but not just
    to be an expiating
    scapegoat.
But before he told them
about that suffering
and of that fight,
he first showed them
the final outcome:
    humanity in its
    glory,
    humanity in the fullness of
    life.
He asked them
to come with him.
They came.
They climbed
that high mountain
to be alone
at its very top,

that end of the earth
where heaven
is met.
    The readings today
    ask us to see
    that trip in the light
    of another group of four men
    climbing a mountain
    too,
    three thousand years
    before:
        Abraham and Isaac,
        two other young men,
        and a donkey
        with wood, fire, and a sword.
They had marched
for three days
before they had come
to the foot
of the mountain.
Abraham told the two:
"You wait here."
He unloaded the donkey
and put the wood
on the shoulders of his son
Isaac,
and they climbed on,
Abraham carrying the fire
and the sword.
    While they were
    on their way to the top,
    Isaac said:
    "My father."
    Abraham said:
    "My son."
    Isaac said:
    "We have fire and wood
    but where is the victim?,"
    Abraham said:
    "God will provide."

Once at the top,
they built the altar;
they put the wood on that offering place,
and then he bound
his son
and he took his sword,
and in the name of God
up went the
sword . . .
    but then
    a voice
    interfered.
A very strange story,
a story that should be read
in its historical context.
    Abraham was no exception
    when he marched off
    with his son,
    that wood, the sword,
    and the fire.
    He was going to do
    what so many had done
    and so many did
    with their first fruit
    in honor
    of God,
    and to be blessed
    even more.
All over the world
sacred mountaintops
and mysterious dales,
swamps, and niches under doorsills
have been filled
with the bones and the ashes
of these offerings,
in the Middle East, in Europe,
China, Africa, and the Americas.
    Abraham became special
    at the moment
    that, listening well,

he heard that voice
that said:
"Do not raise your hand
against that boy."
And the voice he heard,
he later explained,
was God's.
The lesson in all this
was and is,
without any doubt,
that the reality
that should come first
for us
in this world
is *human life*
and nothing else,
not even God,
in the name of God.
When Jesus,
Simon, James, and John
were at the top,
Jesus started to change,
he got brighter and brighter,
brighter even
than the sun:
humankind in the
fullness
of glory.
Heaven opened
and Moses came out,
the human being
who during his life
had had to cover his face
because of its glory;
and Elijah appeared,
the one who at the end
of his life
had been taken up
in fire and light.

A cloud came down,
and in that cloud,
full of heaven's content,
a voice was heard,
the voice of God,
and it said,
pointing at the glory
of Jesus:
>   "This is my son,
>   my beloved,
>   listen to him."
The promise was clear,
the statement too:
>   the whole of heaven
>   turned around him,
>   and turning around him,
>   around the whole of
>   humankind.
>   It was made clear
>   that listening to him,
>   we would be
>   glorious and victorious,
>   fully human
>   and divine
>   like Jesus.
A promise,
because when they looked around
once more
all was normal again
>   —that is to say,
>   it was like before—
they saw no one
anymore
but only him,
Jesus.
>   It was only
>   after that voice from on high,
>   that, climbing down
>   into this world,

he dropped
his first hint
what the cost
of that glory
and fullness
would be.
He told them
not to tell
anyone
what they had seen,
"Until,"
he said,
"I am
risen from the
dead."

17.

HE GOT MAD

John 2:13–25

Jesus
only once
got really mad.
He got mad
in a church,
in the temple.

    When he entered
    the temple
    that afternoon
    to pray,
    he saw the priests
    and the merchants,
    and the cattle dealers,
    and the bankers,
    and the hawkers,
    and the profiteers;
    he saw the rich,
    with their fattened
    sacrificial animals;
    he saw the poor,
    the orphans and the widows
    with their skinny
    pigeons.

        And the thought
        of his mother and Joseph
        came to his mind,

85

who once thirty years ago
had come to that same temple
with him
and a pigeon,
the offering of the
poor.
He remembered
how his mother had told
him
how difficult it had been
to get the money
even for that bird,
and how offishly
they had been
received.
He heard the noise,
the shouting and the hackling,
coins thrown together,
the refusals and the bragging.
He smelled the sweat
of the nervous animals,
their dung
and the rubbish-heaps.
He slipped in the dirt
of the temple square,
        and he got mad,
        very mad.
        He took his belt,
        he lashed out with it,
        he chased them all
        from the temple;
        he freed the cattle,
        slapping them on their shoulders
        so that they stampeded away;
        he opened the cages
        and the pigeons
        flew off
        straight into the sky
        where they belong;

he took fistfuls of coins
and threw them
into the gutters;
he took their tables
and turned them over,
and all the while
he shouted
at the top of his voice:
"Stop all this,
what did you do
to the house of
my Father?
You turned it into
a mess,
a marketplace,
a den of robbers."
His disciples
remembered a psalm
at that moment,
about the zeal
for God's house.
He remembered
much more,
how so many prophets
had repeated
again and again
in the name of God:
"I don't want
your sacrifices.
I don't want bullocks
and sheep.
I don't want
your fruits
and yam-yams.
I don't want
your music
and alleluias.
I want justice
and integrity,

joy,
health,
and life
for all.
I don't need
any fat,
nor proteins,
vitamins,
or roughage;
give it to my children,
the orphans,
the widows,
and the poor,
give it to me
suffering
in them.
That is the worship
I want.
*They are the sanctuary
I built.*"
And he,
in his anger,
shouted at them:
"That is the sanctuary
you destroyed,
you hypocrites
and parasites,
but I will raise
it up
in three days,
wait and see."
He was speaking
about his body,
he was speaking
about us,
all of
us.

18.

COUNSELLING EACH OTHER

John 3:14–21

Nicodemus
came to Jesus
in the middle of the night.
He came with a problem.
He was of the old school of thought
and he came to ask:
"How could I, an old man,
be born again?"
 We find that situation
 in the life of Jesus
 again and again:
 people come to him
 to ask his advice.
The Gospels are full
of them:
 his disciples,
 the Pharisees,
 the Sadducees,
 the scribes,
 the rich young man,
 officers and lawyers,
 and in a sense even a man
 like Zaccheus.
He counsels
them all.

The people around him
all seemed to have problems;
they all seemed to walk around
with a difficulty,
a secret,
with a dark or a blind spot
where they wished
to see.
That was not only true
in the time of Jesus;
it is also true
in these days of ours:
everyone has his problems,
her secrets.
It might be anything:
hearing voices,
being pregnant,
having been to a prostitute,
a drinking problem,
a relationship,
a study that does not work,
anything.
We need others
to see clearly
for ourselves
in our lives.
We all need
clarifications
and advice.
We need
others,
the others
need
us.
Churches,
doctors,
priests,
ministers,

the University administration,
deans of faculties
know this
also,
and that is why
there are very often attempts
to organize
counselling services
for students,
and yet,
in a way,
all that does not seem
to work.
      Some years ago,
      an American priest,
      a Maryknoll Father,
      was attached to this chaplaincy
      by the Cardinal himself.
      He was a specialist
      in counselling.
He opened an office,
he had his office hours,
he put up posters,
he had forms printed;
he was highly qualified
and full of pep,
but after about half a year
he gave up
and closed down,
because only *one* student
had been coming to him
during all that time.
      Such a service
      might have worked
      elsewhere;
      it did not work
      in that way
      over here.

Why not?
An investigation was
made
and the final conclusion
was
that most of the counselling
done here
is done in the peer group
and that most of the counselling
done here
is done informally.

It is you
who do it
among yourselves
in the Central Catering Unit,
while waiting at the traffic lights,
while walking through the campus,
in your room,
late in the evening,
in the middle of the day,
indirectly,
spontaneously,
and sometimes very
efficiently,
but other times
very poorly
indeed.

As you all do it,
or try to do it,
or are asked to do it,
it might be worthwhile
to know
how Jesus did it.

Take Nicodemus:
he came with a serious difficulty
and Jesus
referred him to his own
—Nicodemus's—
background.

Take Zaccheus:
he fell out of that tree
full of discontent
and Jesus
said:
"You are a real son
of Abraham."
            Take that rich young man:
            he asked what he should do,
            and Jesus
            made him recall the commandments
            he knew so very well.
There is in Jesus
a counselling technique
in which he really
never counselled,
or decided,
or advised
by himself alone.
            He always
            referred to the other,
            to what the person in need
            already knew,
            and he asked
            then:
            "Make up your mind
            now."
That is also
how you should do it
if anyone turns to you
openly
or stealthily
and asks:
            "How?
            why?
            what?
            when?
            I am in such a terrible
            knot!"

Refer,
refer,
>   to himself,
>   to herself,
>   but do it to their
>   most profound beliefs.
>   Beliefs they might not see
>   anymore
>   because of that problem,
>   that knot,
>   and you will be able to help
>   them
>   to help themselves.
Someone came to me,
and said:
>   "I am so afraid,
>   I am so afraid,
>   I cannot sleep,
>   I cannot concentrate,
>   everyone is against me,
>   they are after me,
>   are you taping my voice?
>   what did you write down just now?
>   is this room bugged?
>   why did the phone ring?
>   I am hearing voices day and night,
>   why did the bell ring?
>   why did you open the window?
>   they are listening in,
>   do you hear those voices?"
I did not know
what to do,
I did not know
what to say,
but thinking of Jesus' method
I asked:
"Did you ever pray?"
The answer was:

"Yes,
I did."
So I said:
"Let us go to the chapel
and pray."
        That is what
        we did
        and peace returned.
        If the roots
        of our body and mind
        reach down into
        our foundations again,
        we will live by the truth,
        and light
        will come
        again.
        Amen.

19.

ON NOT CLINGING

John 12:20–33

"Unless a wheat grain
falls on the ground
and dies,
it remains only
a single grain,
but if it dies
it yields
a harvest hundredfold."
We all know this saying,
we all know what it means,
but we most times apply it
to the death and resurrection
of Jesus
only.
But that is not right,
and, in a sense,
mystifies
the whole issue.
The saying is true
of so many transitions
in his life,
and it should be true
of so many
in ours.
It was true
at the moment
that he left
Nazareth.

He had been working there
as a carpenter,
a kind of old-fashioned mechanic
just like all the others.
They were doing
their usual jobs
in the usual ways.
They had all reached
   a certain welfare,
   a certain position,
   a certain rank,
   a certain fulfillment,
   a certain identity,
   a certain name,
   a certain respectability,
   a certain lifestyle,
   and a certain satisfaction;
      all of them,
      and then,
      all at once,
      Jesus
      escaped.
All the others
were tightly clinging
to all they had acquired,
to their possessions
and their ways of life.
In fact their clinging
belonged
very much
to that way of life.
And then Jesus said,
that evening before he left:
   "I am going to free
   myself";
   and that meant
   that he was going to die
   to the life
   he had been leading
   up to then.

That saying
about the dying grain
was not only true
of his death and resurrection,
it was also true
at the moment
that he came
to this earth
and left God's life
to be with us,
as Paul wrote:
"He did not cling
to his divine life,
he left it
and he made himself
a human being."
> Brother and sister,
> you might ask yourselves:
> where do I come in?
> You came in;
> we are in
> already.
Jesus did not only leave
his neighbors
in Nazareth behind
when he started
to live
that new type
of life of his;
all of us
stayed
behind.
> He introduced
> a new type of life
> while they stuck
> to the old,
> but we stick
> to the old
> as well.

Did you ever read
that remarkable book by Richard Bach:
ILLUSIONS:
The Adventures of a
Reluctant Messiah?
    It tells about
    a person
    who did what Jesus
    did.
    He did not cling
    any more,
    he became free,
    and almost immediately
    he was
    considered to be
    a Messiah
    by all the others
    because he manifested
    a type of life
    that was so much
    fuller than
    theirs.
    And that is why
    he was shot
    by those who did not want
    to change.
It is Lent.
A time of conversion.
Let us try to find
in ourselves
and within our responsibilities
where *we* might die
to fixed patterns
to live
a fuller life.
    Don't think about
    extra-ordinary things,
    but about
    the ordinary ones.

Is there nothing
that at this moment
hinders you
and that you, nevertheless,
stick to?
Is there nowhere
where you would be able
to enlarge
your circle,
to do some good,
to assist others,
to join something,
to be more fulfilled
and *happier*?
Are you willing
to sacrifice
the boredom
of the life
you are living
now?

In Nazareth
he was the only one
to bring
that sacrifice.
How happy he was!
How much he meant
to others!
What price
he paid!
What fruits
it yielded,
the grain
that died!

20.

HOW DO WE GET RID OF HIM?

Mark 14:1-15:47

What we are doing
these days of the holy week
is to commemorate
what happened to Jesus
two thousand years
ago.
> We do not really do
> what the Jews then did;
> we only remember
> what they did.

It is as if
we use a strategy,
a kind of tactics
to place
Jesus
and what happened
to him
in a very far past,
in another culture,
in the midst of totally different
people.
> We seem only
> to "play"
> and that would be
> a very great pity,

101

because in that way
we will never understand
anything,
and we will come to no
illumination
about ourselves
either.
In Jesus
a new type of human life
had been born
into this world.
    A life new
    from all points of view
    in its relations
        to God,
        to laws,
        to rites,
        to this world,
        to children,
        to women,
        to commerce
        and trade.
That new life
had been born
very near to Jerusalem.
It had been announced
to the shepherds,
to the wise men,
but via them
also to King Herod,
        to the political power groups,
        to the church leaders,
        to the scribes,
        to the professionalists
        and the merchants.
And you remember,
don't you,
how they wanted to kill
that new life
from its very beginning?

How Herod commanded
that all new-born life
in Jerusalem, Bethlehem,
and the rest of the province
had to be killed
in order to smother it,
to nip it
in its very bud?
You remember,
don't you,
how Joseph saddled
a donkey
and how the infant Jesus
was carried on that donkey,
kicking holes in that pitchdark night,
from Jerusalem
into the safety
of Africa?
    Why had they
    to flee?
    What were they
    running from?
It was because
of their jealousy
and their fear.
We all know
about that:
    if anyone among us
    is good,
    we are quite willing
    to praise him,
    to hosannah her,
    to alleluia him,
    up to a certain point.
Did you ever hear
anyone praised
without the
"*but*"
that made his or her goodness
dubious,

suspect,
or odd?
        Someone who is good
        is a threat
        to us,
        because if we accept
        that goodness
        unreservedly,
        we
        should be good
        too.
The good person
is an anomaly,
a monster
that should be
lynched.
        That is why
        he had
        to leave Jerusalem
        on a donkey,
        and that is why
        he decided
        to return
        on that donkey again
        just as he had
        left,
        surrounded by the very same
        dangers.
THEY ALL SHOUTED:
"Hosannah,"
"Alleluia,"
"Blessed be the King,"
etc.,
        but,
        oh, sister,
        oh, brother,
        at the same time
        they were asking themselves
        and each other:

how
do
we
get
rid
of
  him?
Isn't that
somehow
 our question
too,
if we are only
"remembering"
him?

21.

ALLELUIA

John 20:1–9

Easter is his dream
come true;
it is his desire
fulfilled;
it is his community
formed;
it is his love
reigning.
    We usually say
    that he overcame
    sin,
    that he conquered
    death,
    that he undid
    evil,
    that he crushed
    the devil.
But there is much more
to it
than just
that.
    We act as if
    Jesus,
    who rose from the dead,
    came back to take up
    again
    our type
    of life,

the life
we live.
He returned
a different
being,
        not only physically
        walking through doors
        and changing place
        with lightning speed,
        but also
        in another way.
The new life
he had lived
—the cause of his death—
had been certified
now,
guaranteed,
sealed,
approved,
and established
by his Father
here on earth.
        They had killed
        it
        and to be sure
        of that,
        they had even pierced
        his heart
        in a heart-rending
        extra.
They had buried it,
deep in the rock,
with a stone
in front,
some seals
on top
and a couple of guards
next to it.
        But that life
        had come back,

still strange
in this world
to begin with.
But now it is sure
that nothing
will be able
to undo it
anymore.
It will grow
and grow
not as a threat
but as a fulfillment,
a final blessing
to the whole of humankind.
Alleluia.

22.

HIS OPERATIONAL TACTICS

John 20:19–31

In Jesus
God
became flesh,
    with eyes
    of a certain color,
    with spittle
    that could be analyzed,
    with hands and feet,
    with a head and a heart,
    a liver and kidneys
    totally like
    us:
    he got tired
    in the evening,
    nervous
    when he did not eat
    in time;
    he was a man,
    but, of course,
    born from a woman
    who knew whom she carried,
    he was of her constitution,
    he lived on her
    in her womb
    for the normal nine months;
    he was born
    from that womb
    and suckled her breasts.

He assumed
our whole human condition.
Through him
God crept
into all the dimensions,
the heights and the depths,
of the human mind
and its flesh.
He touched it
all.

>   That is important,
>   because it was his touch
>   that healed,
>   saved,
>   and redeemed
>   and anything
>   not touched by him
>   would have remained
>   sick,
>   helpless,
>   and bound.

That principle,
a very spiritual
and logical one,
was once expressed
by a wise old saint,
Gregory of Nazianzus,
when he wrote:
*"What was not assumed
was not redeemed."*

>   Brothers and sisters,
>   we should understand this,
>   because only then
>   can we grasp
>   the extent of
>   our mission.

>   >   He touched it all:
>   >   *sin:*

>   >   >   your sins are
>   >   >   forgiven;

sickness:
   stand up and
   walk;
violence:
   put that sword
   away;
prostitution:
   allow her
   to touch me;
children:
   let them
   come to me;
marriage:
   you became
   one flesh;
death:
   he died and
   is alive;
   there is no human area,
   no human sphere,
   he did not touch,
   none.
That is why
he was
and is
   Priest,
   Prophet, and
   King,
and every time
a person
is baptized into that life
of his,
he is anointed
like Christ:
   Priest,
   Prophet, and
   King.
This sounds very lofty,
and that is part
of our trouble.

We should not forget,
that Jesus
exercised
his priesthood,
his prophecy,
and his kingship,
  in his own community
  in his direct daily contacts,
  in his compassion
  for very particular cases:
    that man,
    that woman,
    that girl,
    that boy,
    that tension,
    that wealth,
    that poverty,
    that fight,
    that situation;
and sometimes he was so tired
that he felt
that he should be left
alone.
  That is,
  brothers and sisters,
  how
  we are sent
  into this world,
  WE:
    "As the Father sent *me*
    so I am sending *you*."
When he said this,
he was not speaking
to Peter alone.
  How would Peter alone
  have been able
  to manage a mission
  like that?
He did not speak
to anyone alone;

he spoke to *them,*
his disciples,
that community,
that group
of men and women.
He told them:
go out,
serve,
change
the world,
touch it all
with the Spirit
I will give
you,
> and because we are so many,
> with so many gifts and graces,
> we will be able
> to touch it all:
>> sickness,
>> tension,
>> prostitution,
>> social evils,
>> dangerous transport systems,
>> labor frictions,
>> breaking families,
>> underfed children,
>> sinful housing,
>> insufficient care,
>> lack of ethical values,
>> atomic power,
>> and the silicone chips.

Brothers and sisters,
why do you think
and plot,
why do you buy
and sell,
why do you work
and rest,
why do you run
and rush,

why do you suffer
and have pain:
    is it only
    to help yourself
    to the things
    of this earth,
    or is it to serve
    the new world
    to come:
    HIS WORLD?
"The whole group of believers
was united, heart and soul.
No one claimed for his own use
anything that he had,
as everything they had
was held in common."
    Sent out
    like he
    was sent.

23.

WORDS FAIL

Luke 24:35–48

Jesus was talking to the
two companions.
Did you know that the word
"companion"
means
people who have their
"panis,"
their bread,
together?
      He was talking
      and talking
      and talking.
      He explained to them
      the whole of the
      Old Testament;
      he did not talk to them
      about the New Testament
      because that had not been written
      as yet.
They got sufficient material
to pass their O-levels in OT,
and their A-levels in OT,
and their B.A.,
and their M.A.,
and their Ph.D.
in Bible Studies
and yet,

they did not recognize
him.
They understood,
maybe,
but they did not
see.
> They asked him to stay.
> He stayed
> and he talked on,
> and they remained blind,
> until he took his bread
> and broke it,
> giving each a piece of it
> and it was
> at that moment
> that they suddenly SAW.
The talk had not helped.
Words had failed.
The sign worked,
and immediately they rose
to go to Jerusalem,
to take up
the new life.
> Signs are very often
> more significant
> than words.
> Words do not help,
> verbosity is useless,
> poetry falls flat,
> prose betrays the issues.
The old prophets knew that,
when they had talked their throats
sore,
when they had talked their tongues
out of their mouths,
when they had been shouting
for days and for days
at the tops of their voices,
voices calling in the wilderness,

they would finally
refer to signs
in silence.
     In that silence
     they would crack pots,
     to show the threatening end,
     they would let their vestments
     rot,
     to show the rottenness of the situation;
     they would grow beards
     or their nails;
     they would even,
     as Hosea did,
     marry
     a prostitute
     and start that difficult
     and almost impossible life
     to show that the nation
     had become
     a whore
     in its relations
     with God.
And that Hosea had a son,
and he called him
"Break-the-bow,"
and he had a daughter,
and he called her
"Unloved,"
and he had a second son,
and he called him
"No-people-of-mine."
     And Isaiah,
     that venerable man,
     walked
     as a sign
     of the coming doom,
     naked and barefoot
     for three years
     with, as the sacred text says,

"his buttocks bared"
through the whole of the land.
Let us come back to Jesus
on the way to Emmaus.
His words failed,
his sign spoke.
>   And don't you think
>   that it will be the same
>   in our case?
>   We are no better
>   than our master.
Our words will fail,
the words of all good men and women
will fail,
the words of all the righteous
will fail,
as they have always failed before.
We do not even need the international
conference racket to know that.
>   You might even go a step
>   further.
>   All our prayers
>   failed.
>   We spoke and nothing
>   changed.
>   We prayed and nothing
>   happened.
Everybody is waiting
not for more words,
but for signs:
the breaking of
our bread.
>   That is what we should do
>   in politics,
>   in our education,
>   in our lives.
Jesus talked
and talked
and talked

and they did not
see.
      They did not see a
      thing.
      And then
      he took his bread,
      he broke it
      and they said:
      "IT IS HE."
      They saw
      and straightaway
      they rose
      and a new life
      started.

24.

ONE SHEPHERD ONLY

John 10:11–18

Jesus said:
"I am the good shepherd,
the only one."
And he would add:
"I am the gate,
I am the door,
I am the only entrance,
I am the only exit
that will lead
to anything."
    Our reaction
    to those statements
    can be very different.
    They can be positive
    even to the point
    that we say:
    "In that case
    we should do
    what we can
    to spread that vital piece
    of information."
    They can be negative,
    especially when we think
    about all that has been done
    in his name
    during human history.

I am the good shepherd,
I am the way,
I am the truth,
I am life,
If anyone who rejects me
will die.
> What did he mean?
> What did he want?
> Did he mean
> what Christians mean?
> Did he want
> what Christians want?
> Did he intend
> what Christians called
> so very often
> their
> *Christian ethics?*
> That is a very good
> question!
In 1454 Pope Nicholas V
wrote a decree,
ROMANUS PONTIFEX,
in which he blessed
—in the name of Jesus—
the slave trade.
In 1668
a theologian
at a university wrote
that the justification
of slavery
is a matter of faith
and he quoted
—in the name of Jesus—
> Leviticus,
> the first letter of Peter,
> the first letter to the Corinthians,
> the letter to the Colossians,
> and the letter to Timothy.

In 1864
the Church still had slaves,
and in fact
the first *general* statement
against it
dates from
the Second Vatican Council.
    Study
    Christian church statements
    on the place and the role
    of women in this world,
    even very recent ones,
    and you will be reminded
    of what an old Church Father
    wrote:
        "Women,
        you are the gateway
        of the devil."
We, Christians,
know now
that those statements
    are wrong
    when we read them
    against Jesus' vision.
It is that vision of Jesus
we should test
when we want to know
what he meant
and not the
so-called Christian version
of that outlook.
        It is in his vision,
        that he, seeing the crowds,
        had pity on them,
        because they seemed
        to be scattered,
        to be like sheep
        without a shepherd.

He saw, in a very special way,
how all human beings
belong together;
how we all hang together
—or at least should—
as one tree of life.
    This he expressed
    in his idea of God:
    a Father or a Mother
    and we all
    brothers and sisters.
This he expressed
when his family,
his mother and his brothers and his sisters,
wanted to see him.
But he did not come
because he said:
"Everyone is my mother,
my brother and
my sister."
    This he expressed
    when he handed his bread
    around
    and said:
    "This is my body,
    eat it
    all of you,"
    when he handed his cup
    around
    and said:
    "This is my blood,
    drink it
    all of you"
      as we do now
      during this mass,
      being one,
      without considering
      age or wealth,

social groups, or
the schools where you studied.
This he expressed
when he
in his life
was interested
in all he met:
    the young,
    the old,
    the sick,
    the healthy,
    the dead,
    the sinners,
    the crooks,
    the lost girls,
    and the runaway boys.
It is a vision
in which slavery
is out,
in which exploitation
is out,
in which discrimination
is out,
in which apartheid
is out;
    it is an outlook
    in which the human family
    is really one family,
    in which peace will reign,
    conflicts will be solved,
    and no war will destroy us.
    His vision
    is the only one
    that can save us,
    and that is why
    HE,
    living that vision
    through passion and death
    into resurrection and glory,

is the only way
and the only door,
leading
in and
out.
Let us never forget
that twice
prophets thought
that we Christians
had lost that vision,
at least
in the practice
of our lives.
        Mohammed,
        almost fourteen hundred years ago
        started a new *jamaa,**
        a new human family,
        because the Christians he lived with
        did not want him,
        nor his people.
        Karl Marx,
        more than a hundred years ago,
        started his commune,
        because he doubted
        that Christians
        with their belief
        in God,
        could do it.
They both made
a mistake.
They thought
that Jesus
was at fault;
he is not,
but his followers
were.
        He remains the only
        good shepherd,
        the gate,

the only door,
leading
in and
out.
Alleluia.

*The Swahili word for family, society, company.

25.

A FAMILY THEOLOGY

John 15:1–8

In one of his sermons
the Reverend John Gatu,
one of Africa's Church leaders,
recently said
that theologians all over Africa
were too exclusively speaking
in terms of
a liberation theology
only.
    He did not say
    that one should not preach in terms of
    a liberation theology.
    One should,
    for all kinds of obvious reasons,
    but he said,
    that the Bible,
    after speaking about
        the Exodus,
        the desert period,
        the safari,
        the long march,
        and the great leap forward,
    had developed also
    another theology,
    or even theologies:
        a theology of after the arrival,
        a theology of consolidation,

127

a theology of settling,
a theology of work,
a theology of organization,
a theology of growth,
a theology of building a new home,
a theology of the family.
And he added,
that this switch-over
had,
to a great extent
still to be made
in this country Kenya:
 making a home,
 or perhaps
 re-making a home.
And Jesus said:
"Make your home in me."
Most probably
this will sound okay
in the ears of many of you.
In the ears of very many others
it might sound
ironic.
 To them it sounds ironic
 for a very serious reason.
 And this very serious reason
 is a very touchy issue
 at the same time.
 Some African scholars
 will explain
 that African societies
 were organized within
 the family context,
 within the context of the
 extended family.
Birth,
initiation,
marriage,
education,

religion,
life,
love,
and death
were all family affairs.
        Any African student
        who ever wrote an assignment
        on his traditional background
        will come to the same conclusion.
        Everything was a family affair.
But that original African family
was completely,
or almost completely
upset
by the things
that happened
in these countries
about eighty years ago,
and one of these "things"
happened to be
Christ
and Christianity.
        And here is
        now
        that invitation
        of Jesus:
        make
        YOUR HOME
        in me.
Who has to make
a home in Jesus?
        Is it I,
        myself?
That is what very many Christians
seem to think:
it is I
who am called.
I and
Jesus.

And the African scholars
we just spoke about
say
that that attitude
is
exactly
one of the reasons
and even one of the main reasons
for the BREAK-DOWN
of the family pattern.
People started to relate
to Jesus,
independent from their families,
independent from their contexts,
independent from their households.
That attitude
does not seem to be very
helpful.
It does not work.
It seems to be wrong.
And it does not seem
to correspond completely
to Jesus' intentions
either.
Jesus said:
"I am the vine,
I am the stem,
I am the trunk,
I am the tree-trunk,
you are the BRANCHES."
Jesus did not say:
"You are the leaves."
Not a leaf,
not a flower,
not one leaf,
not one flower,
but a branch,
a branch.
And a branch is a cluster,
a branch is a collection of things,

a branch is an organized unit,
a branch is a living organism
and that is how
we are supposed to relate
to him—
as a branch.
        Paul, in one of his letters,
        the one to the Romans,
        speaks
        about Jesus being the stem,
        or the trunk,
        or the root.
        And he says:
            all twigs,
            all shoots,
            all branches
            should be grafted
            on him.
Not one leaf.
Who can graft one leaf?
Not one flower.
Who can graft one flower?
But branches,
those family type
of things;
they should be grafted
on him.
        Jesus himself had said,
        that the MASTER,
        and he meant himself,
        should be put
        over the
        household.
And it is maybe
for that reason
that he compared
the kingdom of God
to a householder.
        And Paul baptized:
            the household of Lydia,

the household of Stephanus,
the household of Prisca,
the household of Aquila,
and Peter baptized
Cornelius
and his household.
We should relate
to him from
within our families.
To believe
is
a family affair
and not
an individual
thing.

26.

THE LANGUAGE OF LOVE

John 15:9–17

Jesus says
that he loves us
and that we should love him,
that he is our friend,
and that we are his friends,
and that we should be friends
and love each other
too.
    All this sounds
    very nice,
    but it is very confusing too,
    not only in the reality of our lives,
    but even in the language
    we use.
I know a boy,
an orphan about twelve years old;
he ran away from the household
of a mother with some children
who had picked him up
from the street
to take care of him.
He ran away;
I knew him,
I found him,
and I asked:
"Why did you run away?"
and he got big tears in his eyes
and did not answer.

133

So I asked,
as helpless as he,
"But don't you love Ruth
[the name of his foster mother]?"
And he said:
"Yes."
And then I said,
rather stupidly, I am afraid,
"Do you ever tell her,
that you love her?"
And he looked at me,
frightened,
and he said,
"No."
And I said,
"But why not?"
And he said,
"She would think
that I . . ."
      Brother and sister,
      I am not telling a story;
      it is the truth.
      It is a truth
      Jesus must have experienced
      also
      in his life
      while he tried to explain
      to those
      hard-hearted followers of his
      what he felt
      for them.
Do you remember
how he asked Peter
"Do you love me?"
and how Peter
in fact
gave all the signs
of being extremely embarrassed
by that very simple
question.

Some days ago
there was a farewell party
for the third-years
who are going to leave,
and someone said
at the end of the speech,
"I love you all
very much,"
and there was a snigger
and a laugh.
Why?
It is strange
that we human beings
have developed
a terrific language
to name the external world.
We can name and indicate
everything.
   A car-mechanic
   has a name for all the parts
   of a car;
      a doctor
      has a name
      for every muscle and bone
      in our bodies;
   a musician
   has a name for every part
   of his or her instrument;
      a Nuer cattleholder
      in the Sudan
      has over three hundred names
      to indicate
      the color patterns
      on the hides of cows;
   a pharmacologist
   has a name and label
   for the contents
   of hundreds of bottles;
      but when it comes
      to our internal world,

when it comes
to our emotions, passions,
and feelings,
we seem to fail:
I love you,
I like you.
And that is not
because English
is our second or third
language.
Even those who speak English
as their own mother tongue
have the same difficulty.
Did you ever listen
to the conversation
of two people
who fall in love
in an English-speaking film:
"You are my
fruit salad,
you are my strawberry
with cream on top,
you are my
baby,
my darling,"
and so on.
The difficulty is not
only one of language;
the difficulty is
in our lives.
It is a difficulty
that often makes life
hard and cruel,
savage and shortsighted.
Because of it
some even seem to come
to the conclusion
that marriage
always and everywhere
is a sick joke,

because the girls say:
"The only thing the boys
want is us
stripped in bed";
and the boys say:
"The only thing the girls
want is us,
stripped from all we have,
with empty pockets."
Brothers and sisters,
is this really
true?

    In the reading for today
    Jesus fumbles with our
    human language and
    with our human words,
    but he makes one thing clear:
    we should love one another,
       because God loves us
       and God gave us
       to each other.
It is there
that I meet
a mystery
in you,
and you meet
a mystery
in me,
    indescribable,
    but everlasting.
And it is because
of this
that we should not stop
loving,
and it is because
of this
that we should not stop
suffering
until all suffering
is over,

for,
as an African philosopher
—Aimé Césaire—
once wrote:
"In the whole wide world
no poor devil is lynched,
no wretch is tortured
in whom
I too
am not degraded
and murdered."
Friends
we should be,
friends,
brothers and sisters.

27.

HE LEFT IT TO US

Mark 16:15–20

He had been with them
for forty days.
They had been very glad
to see him again.
But something had changed:
     there are no reports
     on miracles worked
     by him
     during that time.
     Nothing at all,
     except the way
     in which he appeared
     suddenly
     through ceilings and floors
     through unopened windows
     and locked doors.
He spoke to them,
that is true,
but when he spoke to them
he only spoke
about them.
He told *them*
that he was going to give *them* powers,
the power to forgive each other,
the power to cast out evil,
the power to handle with their bare hands
snakes,

those animals that had always been
the symbol of sin.
He told *them* that they would drink
the deadly poison
of this corrupt world
but that they would not be harmed.
He told *them*
that he would send *them*
his holy Spirit.
>   But for the rest
>   NO NEWS;
>   nothing happened
>   until that fortieth day
>   when they met,
>   on a mountaintop.
It seems to have started
with their question,
a question that had been burning
on their lips
and in their minds
for so very long:
>   "Lord, has the time
>   come?
>   When are YOU going
>   to restore
>   this world?"
When they asked
that question
his feet left this earth
a little bit.
>   "When are YOU
>   bringing us
>   the salvation and redemption,
—he got a bit higher—
>   the emancipation and justice,
>   the goodness and integrity,
—he got a bit higher again—
>   the health and the life,

the development and the
Kingdom of God
you have promised,
and we are waiting for?"
—*he was very high now.*
The more they insisted
the higher he rose,
and he said:
    "Let us not discuss
    times and dates,
    let us not discuss
    when it all will be
    finalized,
    but let us discuss
    how you,
        you,
        you,
    will receive the Spirit
    and how you
    will have to go out
    proclaiming the good news
    from here till the end of the earth,
    baptizing those who believe,
    casting out devils,
    picking up snakes,
    using your gift of tongues,
    laying your hands on the sick."
"Start moving
you,
you,
you,
not me:
I am leaving,
it is now
up
to you."
    And while he was saying this
    he left this earth,

getting higher and higher
until they did not see him
any more.
And they went to
Jerusalem
to wait for his Spirit.
Many of us claim to be Christians,
to be the followers
of Jesus Christ,
but how many of us
take the task he left us
seriously?
We are quite willing to pray,
to spend some time in church,
but how many of us
carry our tasks
from that church
into our daily lives?
We live in a world
that is far from good,
we all know about
the snakes,
the sins,
the corruption,
the hunger,
the bribes asked for,
the neglect,
the deception.
But are we not
very often
using Jesus Christ
to sit down more quietly
in this rubble and rubbish
because we say:
"After all
he redeemed us,
we are washed in his blood,
we are safe,
we are saved,"

and we look up to the Father,
and we fold our hands,
and we bend our knees,
and we distribute our Bibles,
and we close our eyes,
and we close our ears,
and we close our noses,
and we close our hands,
and we close our mouths,
and we bless the world,
and we bless even its bombs
and its fighter jets,
and we sing:
    "amazing grace"
and
    "we are not of this world"
and
    "alleluia, praise the Lord."
And insofar as we are concerned
in this world
nothing is going to change,
because we glorify him
who sits at the right hand of
God the Father.
    But,
    brother or sister,
    do you know
    what Jesus Christ
    is doing there
    at that right hand?
    It is explained to us
    in the letter to the Hebrews
    chapter ten, verse thirteen.
    That letter reads:
        "He took his seat
        at the right hand of God
        where he is waiting
        until his enemies
        are overcome by us!"

His disciples
were left by him
here on earth,
because of that.
That is why
he had said:
     "I leave you as
     salt,
     I leave you as
     yeast,
     I leave you
     as light!"
       We often piously think
       that we should be waiting
       for him,
       while in actual fact
       he is waiting
       for us.

28.

YOUR NEAREST ONE IS NAKED

John 17:11–19

In February 1979
a very famous
and infamous
German-American philosopher,
Herbert Marcuse,
became eighty.
He had been the leader
of the 1968 student revolutions
all over the world.
> He has been struggling
> his whole life
> with the idea
> of changing this world,
> of getting rid
> of the actually existing structures,
> of its capitalistic tendencies,
> and of its alienation.
When on his eightieth birthday
other philosophers went
to congratulate
and interview him
he was still thinking
in those terms,

but he said
that he had started to see
that the doctrine of Sigmund Freud
is most probably
more worth our attention
than the one of Karl Marx.
Karl Marx had said
that we should change
this world
and its structures,
that we should change
its economic system,
that we should abolish
practically
the whole existing situation,
our salary- and wage-system,
the competitive educational system,
the marriage customs,
the division into national states,
and so on.
Sigmund Freud, too,
had been thinking
about a radical change,
but he had situated the difficulty,
the snake that poisons us,
not only outside of us
in the world around,
but in the human being.
He had said,
—and now I am obviously
simplifying—
that we in our own hearts and minds
have two tendencies,
the one to make live
and the one to destroy,
the one to be with others
and the one to assert ourselves,
the one in which we love,
and the one in which we kill,

we have a life-wish
and a death-wish.
The old Habermas said
without any reference to Jesus:
"If only
we would be able
to change
the human person
so that its forceful
destructive power
would be put at the service
of its life-giving tendencies."
That is,
my dear friends,
exactly
what Jesus proposes:
that we change
in that way.
He wishes us
to change
internally, psychically,
psychologically, and spiritually,
and he himself
even used the forces
that killed him
to show his love.
He used
the powers he had
not to destroy
but to build
and construct:
his disciples said,
when they were not well received
in a certain village,
"Destroy it and its people,"
but he said:
"No, let it live,"
because he loved them.

When they arrested him
he showed them his power
three times
by letting them fall on their faces,
but he did not destroy them;
he let them live
because he loved them.
He told Pilate
that he could have mobilized
all the armies
in the world of the spirits,
but he did not do it,
because he loved all.
He had changed,
he was
a new human being,
a transmutation.
It is a pity
that Habermas
never seems to have met
him.
> We should acquire
> that same change-over
> by practicing
> that new humanity,
> by loving one another,
> and we should show this our love
> by loving the ones
> nearest to us.
And the nearest to us
is the one
to whom we promised
to give ourselves
fully
and totally,
free and naked
for always
and always.

That promise
made in marriage
is something terrific,
something almost unbelievable,
but also something very delicate;
it puts us
in an extremely vulnerable
position
toward each other.
You are so near
to each other,
you can make the other
grow
if you use
your life-giving power;
but you can murder
the other
if you use
your destructive tendencies.
To give life
in marriage
is not only a question
of genes or of bodily cells;
it is not only a connection
between sperm and ova;
it is too an issue of
giving life to each other,
man and woman,
spiritually and psychologically.
If a husband
tells his wife
all the time:
"You useless creature,
you uneducated clown,
you good-for-nothing,
you blot on my name,"
she is not going to
survive,

and if she has
that kind of attitude
to him
he will not survive
either;
he might fill her womb
with children
and new life,
but he himself
and she too
will dry up
in that harsh
and dry
climate.
You can make
very many mistakes
when you marry
and try to live together.
Some mistakes
are very simple
and therefore, maybe,
so often made:
    there is the mistake
    of not organizing well
    your finances before you marry;
    there might be the mistake
    that you did not build in
    an emotional outlet;
    there might be very many
    other mistakes;
but the main mistake
ALWAYS is
that you don't build
your love
by affirming each other,
but that you destroy
your love
by negating each other.

If I say
YES
to you,
you grow
(and so do I);
if I say
NO to
you,
you die
(and I too).
Habermas said,
eighty years old:
"Find a new
human person."
Jesus said:
"Love one another,"
and he sends his Spirit
of love
to work out
that change,
and sending that Spirit
to us,
he said
YES
to you and to me,
working in us
that possibility
of building a new world,
the new humanity
   everyone
   is
   dreaming
   about.

29.

IDENTIFYING THE NEWNESS

John 20:19–23

The disciples of Jesus
experienced,
ten days after his departure,
that they were changed over
from the people
they formerly had been
to a completely
new human strain.
> They started,
> immediately after the reception
> of the fire and the wind,
> the breath and the life,
> to do things,
> they had never done
> before.
They were new.
This sounds eerie
and mysterious,
abstract and
empty,
as long as we express
all this
in theological
or more or less theological
terms.

Why don't we try
to express it
in another way?
      Why don't we say
      that after that Holy Spirit
      explosion and implosion
      they had made a further step
      in humanity?
      They had entered
      a new dimension.
      They gave signs
      of a new insight;
      they opened in the history
      of human evolution
      a new period,
      a new era.
And after having decided
this
we should then try
to identify
that newness!
We should try to
isolate it
for a moment
      from the older ways,
      from the older insights,
      from the older attitudes.
We very often hear
about beginning
new eras and new periods
in human life.
      Every time
      a new region
      in Kenya
      gets piped water
      or access to electrical power,
      the District Commissioner
      or the member of Parliament
      of that constituency

will address the *wananchi**
and speak in terms
of a new era,
    a new start,
    a new creation,
    a new epoch;
but in fact
human life
in its relationships
goes on
as it has always
been going on before.
The only difference is
that the quarrels at home,
the fights in the bars,
the deceptive talk
is now done
in electric light
while drinking
clean water.
    Real human newness
    cannot be
        a building,
        a power plant,
        a landing on the moon,
        a flight to Mars,
        a psychological theory,
        a sociological paradigm,
        a new communication system,
        or anything like that.
You cannot change
the quarrels in a family
by eating better food,
by installing a television set
or by buying a larger car,
or some presents
for your husband,
your wife,
and your children.

A real evolutionary step,
real progress
can be made only
if mentalities
and attitudes,
if outlooks
and judgments
change.
That is what happened
at the moment
that the Spirit descended,
at the moment
that all his disciples
became not only capable
of speaking all kinds of languages
but were willing to use
those languages
to contact people
they would never have thought
of addressing before.
That newness came
not so much at the moment
that Jesus breathed over them
and said:
"From now on,
you will be able to forgive
sins,
and evil
done to you,"
but at the moment
that they did forgive
each other,
at the moment that they
did not relate to one another
any more
as enemies and competitors,
as rivals and contestants,
but as parts
of one humanity.

Brother and sister,
you know
how old-fashionedly
we relate to one another.
>   Almost all of us
>   see our fellow human beings
>   automatically
>   as threats.
>   That is why Cain killed
>   Abel
>   from our very beginning.
>   Every time we meet
>   someone new
>   we almost instinctively
>   put our hairs
>   up.
You know
how, notwithstanding
all the words and the smiles,
we live in a competitive world
even in our schools
where children are taught
to fight and push,
to be first
and exclusive.
>   You know
>   how the apparent order
>   in this world
>   is based on
>   murder and violence.
You know
how the power balance
here on earth
is based on weapons
that can destroy
all of us.
>   You know
>   about nuclear power,

about the lie
that only the further development
of those destructive powers,
directly directed against us,
can save us!
You know how President Carter
when taking his oath as President
spoke of:
    "Eliminating nuclear weapons
    from the face of the earth,"
and how he said
hardly two years later:
    "Our deterrent is overwhelming,
    and I will sign no agreement
    unless our deterrent force
    will remain overwhelming."
If we want
a new humankind,
all that should change.
If we want to survive
as human beings
in a human society,
we will have to jump out
of those attitudes.
        Not only nationally
        and internationally,
        but also
        and maybe even more so
        in our personal relations
        from man to man,
        from woman to woman,
        from man to woman
        and from woman to man.
When we intend to use
violence and destructiveness
against one another
we don't even intend
to live as human beings.

Did you ever notice
that you cannot beat or kick
a fellow human being
without declaring him or her first
to be a beast?
"You are a pig,"
the policeman says,
and then he kicks.
"You are a swine,"
the public answers,
and then beats
the police.

> *That is the reason*
> *why for us human beings*
> *the Association for the Prevention*
> *of Cruelty to Animals*
> *is so important.*

I read a "poem"
while invigilating
an examination in Ed 120,
a poem scratched with a ball-pen
on a desk:

> "Oh baby, oh baby,
> when you kiss me
> my mind fills with desire,
> you are my sweetest—*thing.*"

If that is true,
if you are a thing,
I can do
with you
whatever I want.
But it is not
true.

> The newness of Pentecost
> is a newness in human relations,
> it is a peace-feast,
> and that is how Jesus
> introduced it.

It is a communication-feast,
an antidestruction celebration,
a we-belong-together demonstration,
a forgiveness occasion:
an evolutionary step.

Wananchi: the Swahili word for "citizens."

30.

TRINITY TRACES

Matthew 28:16–20

It must be clear
to any one of us
that we touch in the feast of
the Blessed Trinity
on a mystery,
     a secret,
     a riddle,
     a drama.
As soon as you start
to try to understand
a person,
any person,
even yourself,
you bump
into that very same type of
difficulty.
     Can you explain yourself
     to yourself?
     Can you explain yourself
     to someone else?
Is there any father or mother
who really understands
his son or her daughter?
     Who can fathom
     the human heart,
     who can understand
     the human mind?

Who can measure
his emotions
or her complexities?
      NO ONE.
      And who would be able
      to know God?
      Not a human being
      in this world.
      NO ONE.
And that is,
if you think of it,
terrible;
it is fearful
especially because that unknown
other one,
GOD,
has power over life and death,
over our life and our death,
power over the standing of the trees,
and power over their falling down,
power over thunder and lightning,
power over storms and rains,
power over the moon and the stars,
power over the animals and all that lives.
      It is no good,
      it is frightful
      not to know anything
      about a person
      who has power over
      you;
      what kind of man is he,
      what kind of woman is she?
Students who have to sit
for oral examinations
will try to find out,
desperately,
about their examiners:
      what do they look like?
      what are their preferences?

what are their hobbies?
are they married?
do they have children?
are they believers?
should we shake hands?
how should I dress,
   very nicely or a bit
   slovenly?
what color would they like?
do they drink?
do they smoke?
And that other student,
who has been arrested
because of one or another mishap,
a very stupid one,
will also try to find out:
what court have I to go to,
Kibera or Makadara?
what courtroom shall I be in,
one, two, or three?
who is going to be the magistrate?
what kind of man is he?
how should I approach him?
does he like people to wear ties
or does he prefer them without ties?
should I put on my jeans,
or should I wear a pinstriped suit
like the attorney general?
should I plead guilty,
like an almost butchered lamb
or should I proclaim my innocence
like a roaring lion?
     And yet all those
     are only human beings
     made of our own flesh and blood;
     their power is great
     but always somewhere restricted;
     but what about God?

On God
we depend totally
and integrally
in our lives and
in our deaths.
We will have to appear
before him,
our final examiner,
our last judge,
at our transition
from this life to that
other life,
at the moment
that we are born
from this world,
our common mother,
into God's lap,
on the knees of our common
Father,
who then will inspect
and test us,
giving us our final
eternal name.
        Who is God?
        How is God?
In a way,
Jesus of Nazareth,
that person that many of us
call
the anointed one:
Christ,
did not reveal anything else
but that.
He revealed to us
who God is
and how God is.
        He revealed to us
        that God is community,

that God is not alone,
though one,
that God is family,
that God is not isolated,
that God is not aloof,
haughty, or unsociable,
that God relates,
that God loves,
that God is *one,*
yes,
but *many*
too.
That God is not sitting alone
on a throne
hard like a diamond,
blinding like the sun,
cold like crystal,
majestic like a dictatorial ruler.
God is a life-process,
God is a parent
and a child
and their love.
A loving loved lover
doubly loving doubly loved lovers,
because that is what it means:
TRINITY.
   But theologians
   were not content,
   even knowing all this,
   and they tried to find out
   more about that life
   from which we all
   are born
   and from which we all
   are carrying *the seed* and *the spirit,*
   and they asked,
   "What do they do,
   those three in one?"

They found the answer
and they used a Greek word,
a beautiful one:
epichoresis,
and that means
a *dance:*
they are dancing
hand in hand,
three in one,
enjoying each other,
enjoying their lives.
> If that is true
> and if we are their children,
> it should be true of us
> also.

If that is true,
then that dance
must be their kingdom
and their power,
and it should be our kingdom
and our power
too.
> If that is true,
> then that dance
> must be the core
> of their divine culture.

And it is especially
here in Africa,
here in Kenya,
that this intuition
gets a very special significance.
> How often
> did not
> the late president of this country,
> Mzee Jomo Kenyatta,
> say
> that the core of African culture
> is the *dance.*

Not the dance around
something,
not a dance around
a golden calf,
but the dance
in which men and women,
the old ones and the new ones,
enjoy and dance and celebrate
their lives
together in peace
and without fear
in community,
not thinking of themselves
alone.

> To be able to live
> that life,
> to be able to dance
> that song,
> we must be like
> them,
> those three in one,
> without fear of one another.

The seed and the spirit
are planted
in all of us
—traces of Trinity—
and one day they will break
through
and off we will go
citizens of God's kingdom,
participants in God's family life,
companions,
brothers and sisters,
born to dance together.

31.

BEFORE AND AFTER CHRIST

Mark 14:12–16, 22–26

The story of today
brings us to one of the last days
in Jesus' life.
His followers did not yet seem
to understand
that he had come to bring
a change-over.
They were only thinking
about a repetition,
a glorious repetition
of the past.
    So they asked him,
    at the last Easter during his life,
    "Where do you want *us*
    to make the preparations
    for *you*
    to commemorate
    the Passover feast?"
They were willing
to celebrate with *him*
under *their* direction
the commemoration of the fact
that long, very long ago
the Jews had been liberated
from Egypt
by God.

167

They were willing
to celebrate with him
that ancient happening
according to the old law
and according to the set
customary rules.
That is what they
wanted to arrange.
But even without saying so
explicitly,
Jesus took
the initiative
from the very beginning.
First there is that man,
that strange man
carrying a pitcher of water
on the top of his head,
an activity that up to then
only women
had been seen
doing.
Was that man
maybe
already a sign
of the new deal
that was going
to come,
a sign of the barriers
falling away?
They have to follow
that man
and then ask the master
of that house
in his, Jesus' name:
"Where is *my*,
that is, Jesus' dining room,
in which I, Jesus,
can eat with *my* disciples
the Passover meal?"

And after he had taken over,
he stuck
to his initiative:
as they were eating,
he took some bread,
he broke it
and gave it to them,
then he took his cup
and he gave it to them
also.
      They were amazed
      that he broke,
      without any further ado,
      the most sacred
      and the most set rite
      of their lives.
      They wanted a repeat
      of the old story,
      he gave them the beginning
      of the new sequel.
Even later,
after his death and resurrection,
we have a report
on his singular behavior.
He had walked
with those two fellows
from Jerusalem to Emmaus.
      That story does not say
      that he went with them
      to their home,
      most probably because those two
      did not go
      to a place
      they as Jews could call their home.
      They went to Emmaus,
      a place
      that in the time Mark wrote
      was nothing else
      but a large settlement,

the Roman barracks,
where they worked
as servants.
That is why those two
especially
had hoped so much
that that whole colonial period
would have been finished
by Jesus.
They invited him
to join them
at table.
He accepted
after some apparent hesitation.
They were his hosts,
he was their guest,
but there too
he immediately
changed those roles.
He, the guest,
took the bread,
he, the guest,
broke it,
he, the guest,
gave it
to
them.
They had resigned
to the old way,
he started
a new one.
And they suddenly saw
and believed
and jumped up
and walked
through the night
and the dangers of robbers
and police

back to Jerusalem
to say
not only
that they had seen
HIM,
but also
to tell
that he had
done it
AGAIN:
a new pass-over,
indeed,
a new economy,
indeed,
a new technology,
indeed,
a new human being,
indeed.
But let us look not only
at his bread
and his wine,
let us
look
at him on the cross.
It was on that cross
that human history
was broken into
two:
before
and
after
Christ.
It is that vertical beam
with him on it
that divides
the horizontal line
of our human history
into two.

That beam
and his death
divides the old from the new,
the right from the left,
the world as it was and is
from the world that is going
to be.
It is the line
that we should draw
through our own lives
too.

32.

EVERYONE A PROPHET

Luke 1:57–66, 80

If there was ever a prophet,
then it was John the Baptist.
   John was announced
   in a prophetic way:
   while his father Zacharias
   was serving in the temple,
   an angel appeared
   and said:
   "You and your wife are going
   to get a son."
   Zacharias could not believe it
   and he said so:
   "I am old and my wife
   is well on in years."
   The angel answered:
   "Your son you are going to get,
   but because you did not believe it
   you will remain speechless
   until he will be born."
John was conceived
in a prophetic way:
life was born
from a dead womb,
from a dead world.
   John lived in that womb,
   in that world,
   in a prophetic way,

173

because when his mother
bearing him
met Mary,
it was John
in that old aunt
who jumped up
and made her, Mary,
carrying the new world,
known.
He was born
in a prophetic way
because his father
who had been dumb
    for nine months
    suddenly started
    to speak again.
John grew up
in a prophetic way,
because, while all the others
got their normal formal education
in the world in which they lived,
John grew up in the wilderness,
getting his new insights
directly
from God.
    John dressed himself
    in a prophetic way
    because while all the others
    were worrying about fashion
    and about having themselves washed
    and perfumed three times a day
    he walked around
    in a camelskin
    with a leather belt.
John ate
in a prophetic way
because he did not touch
any processed food at all
but ate things
as they came from God,

straight from heaven:
honey and insects.

    John knew
    in a prophetic way
    because he could discern
    what was old
    and what was bad,
    and he pointed as the first one
    at the newness that appeared
    in Jesus.
John was active
in a prophetic way,
because he spent his public life
baptizing those
who were willing
to get from the old
into the new.

    John respected life
    in a prophetic way,
    because everywhere
    it was threatened
    he upheld its rights
        against the profiteers,
        against the swindlers,
        against the smugglers,
        against the army,
        against the police,
        against the ruling class,
        against the king,
        and against the so-called queen.
John died
in a prophetic way
because in a time
when hardly anybody ever
really used their heads and their senses
he used his
to the extent that they felt
that his head was so out of place
and strange
that they chopped it off.

Jesus said that John
closed a period,
the old days of prophets
like
Isaiah,
Jeremiah,
Ezechiel,
Elijah,
and all the others.
Their time is over.
The time of those
outstanding, singular cases
is past,
but not because prophecy
disappeared,
but,
on the contrary
because prophecy,
once the mission and task
of few,
is now the task and mission
of all.
Peter understood that
already the first day
of Pentecost
when he said:
"This is what the prophet
spoke of:
God says:
this will happen in the last days,
I will pour out upon everyone
a portion of my spirit,
and your sons and daughters
shall prophesy,
your young ones
shall see visions
and your old ones shall dream
dreams.
Yes, I will endow
even my servants,

      both men and women,
      with a portion of my spirit,
      and they shall prophesy."
That is why,
when celebrating
John the Baptist,
we should not forget
that portion of the spirit
that is in us;
      we are, like him,
      but in a new time,
      prophets.
And that is why
we
in this old world
have to speak
in the name of God,
in favor
of real human life,
as John did.
      In the way we marry
      or don't marry,
      in the way we dress,
      in the way we drink,
      in the way we eat,
      in the way we live,
      in the way we work,
      in the way we relate,
      and in the way we die.
It is up to all of us,
not only to some,
our leaders,
our priests,
or our nuns,
to be prophets
and Jesus did not even hesitate
to suggest
that all of us
should be greater prophets
than John.

John lost his head
on a silver tray
carried by an excited girl
because that night
he
as a prophet
was alone.
The only new one
in that damned old
world.
We should not be alone
anymore.
If we all had played
our prophetic roles,
this world would have changed
more,
very, very long
ago.

33.

HE AND WOMEN

Mark 5:21–43

The gospel reading of this Sunday
contains two totally different reports.
> One is about that embarrassing woman,
> who had been bleeding
> for twelve years.
> She had gone to doctors
> all that time,
> and she had lost
> all her money,
> making that endless circuit
> over and over
> again and again.
The second report
is about a younger woman,
in fact a child,
the daughter of Jairus,
whom Jesus recalled
from what they had called
her death,
and from what Jesus had called
her sleep.
> The preacher can choose
> between the two stories,
> and it is, of course,
> very tempting to leave
> that bleeding lady a bleeding lady
> and to avoid all the embarrassment
> involved

and to speak
on the faith and the love of Jairus
or about Jesus' love for children,
or about those famous words:
"talitha kum!"
meaning:
"Little girl, I tell you,
get up."
If we do that
we miss again the chance
to say something about an issue
that seemed to be
very near to Jesus' heart,
namely,
the place of women
in our human society.
    I don't know
    whether you,
    male or female,
    are well informed
    about the place of women
    in the society
    and in the time
    that Jesus lived.
I don't even know
whether you have ever reflected
about the place of women
in the society
and in the time
that you live.
    I do know
    that the women
    who are described
    in the gospels,
    give,
    they themselves,
    very clear indications
    of their place
    and their role.

Most of the women
speaking to Jesus
excuse themselves
for doing so.
They were in their society
not
allowed to speak to him
just like that.
A woman was
not
supposed to approach a "rabbi"
at all.

Then there is the case
of that other woman
who, praising Mary,
his mother,
reduced her
with the best of intentions
to
how people saw women
in that time.

She hailed her,
seeing him:

"Happy the WOMB,
that carried you!
Happy the BREASTS
that suckled you!"

Immediately
he turned round
to her
and said:

"Don't speak
about my mother
like that:

happy her womb,
happy her breasts.

Stop reducing her
to her reproductive
functions!

No,
happy any PERSON
who listens
to the word of God!"
Henrik Ibsen
wrote, one hundred years ago,
in 1879,
a play
that became famous
all over the world:
A DOLL'S HOUSE.
In that play two persons
are talking:
　　Helmer says to Nora:
　　　"Before anything else
　　　you are a woman and a mother."
　　Nora answers:
　　　"I don't believe that any more.
　　　I believe that I am,
　　　in the very first place,
　　　a human being,
　　　just like you."
　　He:
　　　"You are talking like a child,
　　　you don't understand anything
　　　of the society in which you live."
　　She:
　　　"That is true, I don't understand it.
　　　But from now on I will go on to try
　　　to discover who is right,
　　　society or I."
The woman of the gospel of today
excused herself
for having touched him
not only because she considered
herself unclean,
but because she knew
that according to the ruling
of that time,

after the touch,
Jesus too,
would be unclean
for a week.
      To be a woman
      was no good thing
      in those days.
      Women were unclean
      for seven days after their period.
      They were unclean for seven days
      after having given birth to a son
      and fourteen days after having given birth
      to a daughter.
They were not allowed
to enter any place of worship
for another thirty-three days
after the birth of a boy
and for another sixty-six days
after the birth of a girl.
      The day a girl was born
      meant bad news to the mother,
      because she would be restricted
      for eighty days,
      after which she had to bring
      a sacrifice
      to be "purified."
The lady of today's Gospel
was *always* restricted
because of her bleedings,
and she was desperate about it,
and in her desperation
she did the forbidden thing:
she touched him,
and she was HEALED,
but instead of whooping
and shouting with joy,
she tried to get away
without being seen,
but then he called her back,

and she approached him
in fear and trembling:
"Forgive me
for wanting to be healed;
forgive me
for being a woman;
forgive me for having
touched you;
forgive me for
bothering you;
forgive me for
having made you unclean;
forgive me;
forgive me!"
But he only said:
"My daughter,"
he said:
"Your faith has restored you
to health;
go in peace."
And not a word was heard
about that old law.
No step was taken because
of his legal defilement.
Not a word,
not a word!
The impact
reached much further
than just this healing,
the bleeding
that stopped.
It meant a total
change-over.
A miracle in the
moral and legal
order.
A miracle so deep
that we,
neither men nor women,

even now
risk to go
so far:
      admitting in all we do
      and in all we don't do
      that we are equal
      in everything,
      notwithstanding
      the difference
      that makes
      our equality
      fruitful.

34.

NOT LIKE A PRIEST

Mark 6:1–6

He came to his hometown Nazareth.
He must have been received
with great curiosity.
The stories about him
had been spreading all over the country,
and they must have been told
most eagerly
in Nazareth.
    During the weekend
    that he was staying with them,
    they invited him
    to their synagogue,
    the one he had been sitting in
    so often during his life.
They invited him
to read.
He took the scroll,
rolled it down
to a text in the prophet Isaiah,
and he read aloud to them:
    "The spirit of the Lord
    is upon me,
    because he has anointed me;
    he has sent me to announce
    the good news to the poor,
    to proclaim release to prisoners
    and recovery of sight to the blind,

to let the broken victims go free,
to proclaim the year
of God's favor."
Mark does not mention
all these details.
Mark only mentions
that they did not want
to listen.
>   There is also a reason given
>   why they did not want to listen:
>   they could not believe
>   that a man
>   who had been living with them,
>   who had been going to school with them,
>   who had been eating and drinking with them,
>   could be so different
>   from them.
But one might wonder
whether that was the real reason.
After all,
they had invited him
to the synagogue;
they had come in such great numbers
because they knew
that he was going to be there.
They had handed him the scroll,
and they had been sitting down
full of expectation
to hear him speak.
>   Luke even mentions
>   in his report
>   that there was a general stir
>   of admiration
>   that morning
>   and that they were surprised
>   by his eloquence.
They liked to hear him,
they loved his oratorical skill,
they admired the way he put things.

There is only one thing
they really could have objected to,
and that must have been
his message.
And I think
that we can even trace the reason
for their disappointment
and even, in the end, their anger.
They had come together
religiously,
they had come together
to pray,
they had come together
for comfort,
they had come together
for consolation,
they had come together
to venerate old sacred texts,
they had come together
to use the old images and models,
they had come together
to sing,
they had come together
to escape,
they had come together
to lie in the lap of God
like a cat in the lap of its mistress.
They had wanted him to sing
their tune,
but nicer;
they had wanted him to play
their melody,
but more melodiously
than they had been accustomed to.
That is why they had come,
and now,
he spoiled it all,
because he took a text
that spoke about this world,

and about what should happen
in this world.
He spoke about the poor
and the good news to be announced
to them,
and they knew perfectly well
what that news could mean to them.
He spoke about prisoners
and about the blind,
about broken victims
and this world.
  He spoke about a change,
  a rebellion.
He did not speak
like a priest.
  Priests speak
  always
  within the existing religious context
  in which they live.
  Priests speak about things
  as they are settled.
  Priests speak about the sacrifices
  to be made.
  Priests speak about the prayers
  to be said.
  Priests speak about the obligations
  to be fulfilled.
  Priests speak about the contributions
  to be given.
He did not speak like a priest;
he spoke like a prophet,
and they did not like him
to do that,
because it would mean too much
of a task
and a bother
to them.
  But, brother or sister,
  let us be honest about it:

we are often facing
the same difficulty
as those people there
in Nazareth.
What do we expect from Jesus?
What do we want to expect
from the religious dimensions
in our life?
What function do we allow
Jesus Christ himself
to have in our existence?
Are we only willing
to accept him in his role of a priest,
who built my way
to God,
who offered his blood
to purify me,
who gave my prayers real access
to God,
or are we also willing
to accept him in his
prophetic role,
asking us
to be with him
in bringing life
to all?
Not only by being pious;
piety alone does not help.
Not only by being kind;
the kind word alone deceives.
Not only by being charitable;
charity alone aggravates the situation.
Jesus was not rejected
because he was pious;
he was not rejected
because he was kind;
he was not rejected
because he was charitable;

he was not rejected
because he was a priest.
    He was rejected
    because he was a
    prophet,
    in word
    and in
    DEED,
        being in that way
        the only road
        to peace
        and justice,
        to growth
        and humanity!

35.

NO SPARE SHIRT

Mark 6:7–13

He called
the twelve.
They had been hanging
around him
too long.
He sent them out
in twos,
giving them the authority
and power
to cast out
evil.
That authority
and power was all
they were allowed to take
with them
next to the bare essentials:
one tunic,
one pair of sandals,
one stick
but no food,
no money,
no luggage,
not even a spare shirt.
Which meant that if they had
that one shirt washed,
they had to wait
to get it dried
before going on.

Why were those
rules given
to them?
>It must have had
>something to do
>with the authority and power
>given to them.
>It was that power
>only
>they should put their trust
>in,
>not in money,
>an impressive suit,
>high platform shoes,
>or a beautiful sash.
They should be
simple and even poor
not to overlook
that gift
they had got
for nothing.
>They were supposed
>to start the new human community
>after the chasing out
>and the healing.
That community too
could be built only
on that authority and power
and on nothing else.
>They were not allowed
>to receive any money,
>>any gifts,
>>any spare food,
>>any luggage,
>>or a new spare tunic
>for their services
>either.
>They were supposed
>to return as they had
>gone:

one stick,
one tunic,
one pair of sandals,
and nothing
else.
No glamor,
no show,
no pretense,
no self-glory,
no palace,
no beautiful dress,
no tassles,
no skull-caps
no mitres:
SERVICE ONLY.
As long as his disciples
were faithful to those prescriptions
in the gospel
everything went well;
they lived their real
status.
But no longer faithful,
at the moment they turned
to the acquisition of money
and food,
extra tunics,
and transport different
from their sticks and their feet,
they lost their real nature,
their mission,
and their real selves.
But that is not only true
of those twelve;
it is true
of us
also.
We all are
in our essence itself
nothing but gifts
from God,

gifts to ourselves
and gifts to others.
That is our power,
that is our authority,
that is our nature
and that is our life.
That is what our model Job
understood,
not while he was surrounded by
          his camels,
          his sheep,
          his cows,
          his vineyards,
          his sons,
          his daughters,
          his watchmen,
          his bodyguard,
          his cupboards,
          his barns,
          his chariots,
          his land,
          and his goods,
but when he was sitting alone
          with a stick
          and a shirt,
          some sandals
          and nothing else,
          on the remains of all that
          once had been
          his.
          That is what we
          will realize
          at the moment
          when we will be
          like Job,
          bereaved of all
          at the moment of death.
All will fall away
except
our dependence on God.

At first an unpleasant
thought,
but in actual fact
    our only hope,
    our only security,
    our only joy,
    our real nature
    itself.
Jesus asks us,
just as he asked them,
to remember that
glorious dependence
not only
in the end,
but now
while living
here in this world.
    The less we think
    of that dependence
    and the more we trust
    in things,
    the greater
    our anxiety
    will grow
    and we will never
    be ready
    to be sent
    by him.

36.

HE WENT ON RETREAT

Mark 6:30–34

Jesus was tired.
His followers were tired too.
They had been preaching
and healing,
but the pressure of that work
had become too much.
They had no time anymore
to eat.
They were interrupted
again and again.
     Every time they sat down
     for lunch
     the telephone rang,
     every time they sat down
     for dinner
     there was a knock
     at the door,
     and breakfast had to be
     skipped
     almost always.
Jesus told them:
"Let us go
out of here,
let us have
a rest,
let us be
by ourselves."
     And they packed up,
     they took a boat

197

—crowds cannot follow a boat—
and off they went.
They left
because they had had enough.
They left
because they were exhausted.
        Most times
        this text
        is used in another way.
        Very many recollection
        and retreat-days
        start
        with this text.
The retreat leader says:
        "You have been so
        busy,
        you have been so
        active,
        you have been so
        distracted,
        you have been so
        hurried,
        you have been so
        emptied,
        you have been so
        scattered,
that you need now
a rest,
a retreat,
a period of prayer,
to fill yourself up
with grace
and with prayer
and with God."
        And even when we come
        together
        here in this chapel
        very many of us
        might pray
        in that way.

We come to be restored,
we come to fill our tank,
we come to be replenished,
we come to refill our reservoir,
because,
as we say,
we got empty
during the week
in the hustle
and the bustle
    of our work,
    of our lives,
    of our meetings,
    of our cooking,
    of our appointments,
    of our lectures,
    and so on.
That type of reasoning
and that type of spirituality
can be the cause
of much misunderstanding.
    It might make us think
    that those periods of prayer
    are the only moments
    of sanctification,
    of blessing,
    and of grace.
And that idea
is wrong.
Moments of prayer
can sanctify us,
oh, yes.
But not only
they.
    When Jesus with his apostles
    arrived at the place
    where they intended to rest,
    the crowd that had followed them
    along the shore of the lake
    arrived too.

They stepped out of the
boat
at the moment that the others
stepped from behind
the bushes,
and there they were
again.
      Jesus said to his followers:
      "You get away,
      take your rest.
      I will take care of them."
      And again he started
      to preach
      and to teach,
      and do you think
      that those activities
      did not sanctify him
      then?
      They were his glory
      and holiness,
      his mercy
      and his dedication.
We are sanctifying ourselves
not only when we are praying;
we are sanctifying ourselves
not only when we fill up
our spiritual tanks;
      we are not even emptying
      those tanks
      when we are serving
      each other.
Don't forget
that in the end
he is
—according to Matthew—
NOT going to ask us:
"How much did you pray?"
but
"How much did you serve?"

The tank of our spiritual life
will not get empty
by our activity;
in fact it will get
fuller and fuller.
A drummer does not lose
his skill to drum
by drumming;
in fact his skill
to drum will improve,
but he might get
very tired.
And it is only when
we can sincerely say
that we are tired
because of those services rendered
in the spirit of God
that we may apply this gospel text
to ourselves
and take a rest
and a good meal,
not to restore our spiritual life
that got lost
    —it did not get lost,
    it could not get lost
    in that way; it grew—
but to be able
to continue
our service and love
again.

37.

ONE SMALL BOY

John 6:1–15

The report
on the miracle
of the bread and the fish
is about what happened
to somebody
who gave all he had.
It is, of course, a story about Jesus
multiplying all that bread and that fish.
But
whose bread did he multiply?
Whose fish did he divide?
  It all started
  with the real hero
  of that story:
  one small boy.
Let us have a look
at the eyewitness report.
There were all those people:
5,000 men and most probably
at least double that number
of women and children.
  It is Jesus who says:
  "What are we going to do?
  How are we going to feed them?"
  Philip knows
  what to do to feed them.
  He says:
  "You just buy the food."

But he adds:
"One piece of bread
for each one in this crowd of 15,000
will cost you at least
16,500 Kenyan shillings;
how are you going to manage
that?"
Then Andrew
gets another bright idea.
He asks the crowd,
"Has anybody any food?"
There is a big hush
and a great silence.
People looked at each other.
There must have been quite a few
with some food,
but they kept their mouths shut.
Nobody admitted any crumb of bread,
or any fiber of fish.
They were afraid
that they were going to loose it.
And then there is that small boy.
He had been looking at Jesus
all the time,
with an open mouth
and a wet nose.
He patted his pockets,
he felt under his shirt,
and he shouted:
"Yes, Sir, over here!"
And out he came with five slices of bread
and two fishes,
small ones,
very small ones,
the ones small boys get.
And the whole crowd laughed.
But Jesus did not laugh.
He took those slices of bread,
he took those two fishes,
and he told the people to sit down.

There was a great noise,
and all sat down.
Only that small boy
was still standing there,
and he was looking
with his eyes full of wonder
at his fish and his bread.
And Jesus gave his fish and his bread
to those big apostles of his,
and he said:
"Divide it among them."
    They said:
    "Divide what?"
    And they looked at the crowd,
    and they looked at the bread,
    and they looked at the fish.
But he said again:
"Just start, will you."
And they started to break
and to break
and to break
until everybody had sufficient
and even more than sufficient.
So much so
that they all still had pieces
in their hands
when their stomachs were full.
    And then Jesus said:
    "Can you please collect
    the left-overs?"
They collected twelve basketsful
and I think that Jesus
gave them to that small boy;
after all,
it was his bread,
it was his fish.
    The people praised Jesus;
    they even wanted
    to make him king.

But I think that Jesus
praised that small boy
who had given all he had.
It is that attitude
that should be king
and in Jesus was.
Those who give
will receive
and will receive in abundance.
When you are asked for something
you think you are unable to give,
think of that small boy
of this story,
and think of the twelve baskets
full of food given to him
because he gave
all he had.

38.

BREAD FOR A NEW LIFE

John 6:24–35

From the moment
he had given them
that bread and that fish
the crowds around him
became larger and larger:
men,
women,
and children.
    Some of them even brought
    extra baskets
    to be prepared
    for the next ovenload,
    for the next netful of fish.
But then Jesus turned to them
and said:
    "You are not looking
    for me;
    you are looking
    for bread."
They came to him
as one goes to a bakery-shop;
they came to him
as one goes to a fish-monger:
    to get bread,
    to get fish,
    in order to sustain
    the life we are living
    as we have been living it

and as we hope to live it
as long as possible,
without any change.
They were like a thief
making a sign of the cross
before breaking the window.
They were like an adulterer
saying a prayer
before closing the curtain:
God make sure that nobody will see.
They were like a murderer
invoking God
while sharpening his knife.
They were like soldiers
asking for a blessing
before starting to shoot.
Jesus refused
to give them that bread;
he refused to cooperate
in the continuation of
their old type of life.
He told them
to look for something else,
for another life.
They said:
"What is that something else,
what are the works we should do,
what is the life we should live?"
Jesus said:
"You should believe
in the one God sent to you.
You should believe in me,
in my lifestyle,
in my way of living,
in my way of relating to others,
in my community,
in my way of being
with this world,
with God,
and with humanity."

But they said,
coming back to their starting point:
"All right,
okay,
we will believe in you,
if you give us
first
bread;
that is what Moses did,
that is why our ancestors
believed in him;
he gave them bread,
he gave them water,
he gave them meat."
And Jesus said:
"That is not true.
Moses did not give them
that bread;
it was my Father
who did that."
  They said:
  "Give us bread,
  and we will believe,"
  but they were still thinking
  about bread
  that would help them
  to continue to live the life
  they were accustomed to live,
  a surface life,
  a handicapped life,
  an old life,
  a life too much
  under the influence of the old
  animal instincts,
  a life with the snake
  crawling through it,
  a life full of violence,
  a life full of greed,
  a life full of oppression,

a life without too much
vision,
the life we all know
so very well.
And then he said,
standing straight up
with all his power,
in a most solemn way:
"I am the bread,
I am the bread
of real life.
I am the bread
of heaven.
If you eat this bread,
you will really start
to live,
and you will never
die."
Companions,
and that means eaters
of the same loaf,
what he meant
that day
is that we should
eat
that bread,
that we should participate
in him,
who realized in himself
a new version
of human existence,
a life without violence,
a life full of love,
a life of total freedom,
a life with the snake crushed,
a life with equal respect for all,
a life with a special interest
in the weak and the frustrated ones,
a life full of vision,

a life still so new
to all of us.
Many of us,
almost all of us,
will go for communion today.
We will eat his bread,
we should eat him,
       not to sustain
       and to continue
       the old life,
       but to pick up
       his new life,
       to have his heart
       transplanted and beating
       in us,
           his heart,
           his mind,
           his love,
           and his life.

39.

HE GOT DEPRESSED

John 6:41–51

Elijah was a mighty prophet
in word and in deed,
it was obvious
that God was with him,
     and yet after some time
     he started to lose his power
     and his might.
     People talked against him
     not in a big way
     but in their small ways;
     they found all kinds
     of petty reasons
     to disrespect him;
     they cast suspicion
     on his intentions;
     they laughed too loudly
     when he made a small mistake,
     when his foot missed a step
     or his lips a syllable.
And all this worked
on that mighty prophet
Elijah.
It eroded slowly
but persistently
his self-esteem,
his self-image.

211

He himself
started to stare
at himself
in a mirror
and he himself
said to himself:
"Who are you,
where do your pretensions
come from?
Who was your father,
who was your mother,
who are your brothers,
who are your sisters?"
    And one day
    he got so depressed
    that he did not see anything
    at all
    anymore,
    and he walked into the bush
    for twelve solid hours,
    and then he sat down
    and he prayed to God
    and he said:
    "Oh, Lord,
    I have had enough,
    take my life,
    I am no better
    than my ancestors,"
    and he lay down
    to die.
Brother and sister,
what happened to him,
happens to each of us:
the world around us,
the members of our family,
our brothers
and sisters,
our friends
and relatives,

and all those others
we meet constantly
are
"putting us down,"
or as they will say,
they are putting us
"in our place,"
        and they will say:
        "Who do you think
        you are?
        Where do you come
        from?
        Do you think you are any better
        than we?
        Do you still remember
        that mistake?
        Do you still remember
        that stupidity?"
And we too
can get so depressed
that we do not believe any more
in ourselves,
and we too
would like
to run away
from it all
and end up in the wilderness
to lay our heads
down
and die.
        In the gospel text
        for today
        we find
        that process
        described
        around Jesus.
He is full of spiritual pep;
he says that he is the bread of life,
the life-model for all.

And then
his listeners
start to murmur
around him
and they say:
"Who does he think
he is?
What does he think
he would be able
to offer us?
Isn't he just the son
of Joseph?
Don't we know
his mother?
Isn't that the one
who got into difficulties
as a very young
girl
because of him?"
But Jesus reacts
and he answers them
(and himself)
by referring
to his origin.
"It is the Father
who sent me.
I saw the Father,
I am coming from
him.
I am the living
bread.
I am from
God."
When Elijah got
depressed,
God sent him an
angel
to get him up
again.

That angel reminded
Elijah
of the origin of his mission
and of the power and might
behind and in it.
When they tried to undo
Jesus
by their rumors and gossip,
Jesus reminded himself
of his origin
and of the power and might
behind and in him.
When we are eroded
in our self-image
as Christians,
as sons and daughters of God,
by the people around us
in this world,
we too should remember
our origin,
children of God,
people loaded with spirit,
loved by a Father,
forgiven,
and sent
on a mission.

40.

EATING HIS FLESH

John 6:51–58

He repeated again
and again:
    "I am the flesh,
    I am the bread,
    I am the life,
    I come from the Father,
    I have seen the Father,
    I was sent by the Father,"
    and so on and on.
It seems a very mysterious,
a very deep,
a very difficult,
and an endless
discussion.
    And yet
    it is a type of conversation
    we all have experienced
    though at another level,
    I am sure,
    from time to time.
There is your son
standing in front of you,
and he smokes
not tobacco
but what he calls
weed,

216

and you talk,
and you talk,
and you want to make him
participate or share in
what you know,
in what you have experienced,
in your wisdom,
    and he remains aloof,
    he remains unapproachable,
    he remains unresponsive
    and you say:
    "If I could only creep
    into your head,
    if you could only look
    through my eyes."
You are standing
in front of your daughter,
that beautiful one,
who comes home
very late
from discos
in which there are all kinds of people
you do not know,
you have no relation with,
you have no community with;
and you talk,
and you talk,
and you weep,
and you implore,
and you tap all your experience,
and you fall on your knees,
and you say:
    "If I could only let you know
    what I know,
    if I could only let you experience
    what I experienced,
    if I could let you feel the bitterness
    I have felt,

if you could only drink the water
I drank."
You are standing
in front of your lover,
and there is a very delicate point,
and it is very important to you,
and he does not see,
she does not understand,
he does not feel,
    and you take her hands,
    and you kiss his eyes,
    and you stroke his back under his shirt,
    and you put your head
    in her lap,
    and you say:
        "If I could only be you,
        then you would see,
        if I could only make you see
        with my eyes,
        if I could only make you hear
        with my ears,
        if I could only make you touch
        with my hands,
        if you could only eat the bread
        I ate,
        if you could only be
        my flesh,
        if you could only have
        my blood."
That is how Jesus
talked
that afternoon
to them.
    He knew
    that only his type of life,
    loving,
    forgiving,
    community building,

taking children as your first issue,
simple,
non-violent,
always ready to dialogue,
never hardened,
God-fearing,
human life-respecting
could save
this world
and humankind
from ever-growing
disaster,
    and he pleaded:
    "Please,
    see my point.
    I know.
    Please,
    hear my point.
    I am sure.
    Please,
    feel my point.
    I come from on high:
    eat my bread,
    drink my water,
    eat my flesh,
    drink my blood."
He pleaded
with them,
he pleads
with us
to change,
to see the need
for change.
    To give an example
    of that need:
    Do you know that in 1973,
    in a country like Nigeria
    9 dollars per head were spent on arms,

1 dollar per head on health,
and 3 dollars per head on education?
And in "God's own country," the U.S.A.,
respectively
373, 171, and 348 in the same year?
Think about Jesus
pleading
in his time,
but how would he plead
now in this world,
     in Uganda,
     in Southeast Asia,
     but also
     in Germany,
     in Nicaragua,
     in Lebanon
     and everywhere?
We should eat him,
we should drink him,
     and that is what we do
     but it is as if we are not serious
     about him at all,
     we fragment him
     to nothing,
     to a paper-thin wafer,
     and we reduce his drink
     to a drop of wine.
When eating
his bread
we should feel
what we do,
we should be obliged
to eat a whole loaf
here on the spot,
so that it becomes
an arduous,
a difficult,
and a *felt* task,

in order that we might
turn really
into him,
full of him,
because that is
what we need
and this world
too
and that is what
he knew
so very
well.

41.

SCIENCE, TECHNOLOGY, AND HE

John 6:60–69

Jesus spoke about the flesh
and the spirit.
He seems to separate
two things in us;
he seems to put them apart.
And that is strange,
because we are not two
but only one.
     He spoke about
     the flesh
     that has nothing
     to offer
     and the spirit
     that gives
     life.
Very many people
in the past
have been reading
this text and
coming to very strange
conclusions.
They said:
     "What is my flesh?
     My flesh is my body.
     What is my spirit?
     My spirit is my mind.

As that flesh is useless
and that spirit is all;
I had better try to turn
into spirit alone."
They called their body
a donkey,
and kicked it;
they called it a prison,
and they tried
to escape from it;
they called it the cause of their sins,
and they mortified it,
beat it,
starved it,
tortured it,
did not use it,
and regretted it
very much.
Would that be
what Jesus meant
when he said
that the flesh
on its own
has nothing
to offer?
Jesus, who was accused
of the fact
that he did not fast,
that he did not even teach
his disciples
how to fast.
Jesus, who was condemned
because he was seen
with women
and who enjoyed being
with children.
Jesus, who produced
all that wine in Cana
and all that bread
and all that fish.

He must have meant
something else;
he could not have meant
to say
that our bodies
are only occasions of sin.
Most probably he meant
exactly
the opposite
of what those strange and dated
saints thought.
He did not mean
to say
that we should separate
flesh and spirit,
body and mind;
he intended to say
that we should
never do that,
NEVER.
He wanted to say
that if we separate
those two
we are heading for trouble,
we are doomed.
He said that flesh
on its own
is dead:
a body of a man
in a coffin
is flesh alone;
the body of a woman
in a coffin
is flesh alone;
the body of a girl
in a coffin
is flesh alone;
the body of a boy
in a coffin
is flesh alone.

As long as we live,
the two,
flesh and spirit,
should be together.
      But is that not
      always the case
      as long as we live?
In our body,
maybe,
yes,
but in what
we do
very often
NO.
      Let me give you
      an example.
      In 1633
      some scientists
      met in France;
      in 1646
      a similar group
      met in London;
      in 1660
      some experts
      met in Florence.
They started
scientific societies.
They wanted to invent,
to improve,
to develop,
to progress,
and to be useful
scientifically,
      but they all said
      in their constitutions
      that they
      were not going
      to meddle with
      "divinity, metaphysics, morals,"
      and items like that.

They wanted to study science,
>physics and chemics,
>copper and iron,
>techniques and skills,
>atoms and their explosions,
>biology and ballistics,
>aerodynamics and medicine
>and all kinds of other things
>WITHOUT TAKING INTO ACCOUNT
>THE SPIRIT.
That is what Jesus
warned against,
and we,
living under the threat
of all those scientific developments,
might understand
now
better than even before
how right
he was
and is.
>What should this text
>about the useless flesh
>mean to us?
Insofar as the University
is concerned,
it was explained to us
only two days ago
when the vice-chancellor
said:
>"Scientific research
>is useless
>and dangerous
>when we don't
>at the same time
>do research
>on the moral,
>ethical,
>and religious implications."

Insofar as we ourselves
are concerned,
it means
    that you are wrong
    when you admit
    in your life
    items of flesh
    that are separated
    from the spirit,
    and that wild-growth
    exists in you
    when you say:
        business is business,
        procedure is procedure,
        research is research,
        administration is administration.
It is the spirit
that gives life;
the flesh has nothing
to offer.
Its only offer
is
death,
a body
in a coffin,
a corpse.

42.

RELIGION AND RITUAL

Mark 7:1–8, 14–15, 21–23

Once
there was a man
who wanted to feel safe during the night
in his bed.
That is why he bought
a big lock,
and he put it on his door.
He closed that door every night
with that lock
before he went to sleep.
But after some days
while he was in bed
he doubted whether he had
really
locked the door.
He came out of his bed
to check.
It was locked.
He went to bed again,
but then he thought,
"Did I really lock it?"
and he got out of his bed
and he checked.
It was locked.
He went to bed again
but then, again, he thought:
"Did I really, really check?"

and he got out of his bed
and he checked again.
  That started to happen every night
  and in the long run,
  he could not fall asleep any more
  before he had checked
  three times.
  He knew it was nonsense,
  but he could not sleep
  without that nonsense;
  he had become very
  superstitious.
  He was no longer concerned about his safety
  —all this had nothing to do with his safety—
  he was concerned about a rite,
  a very strange ritual.
Once
there was a lady
who, when she brought a letter
to the letterbox,
put the letter in
and felt
through the opening of the letterbox to see
whether the letter really fell in.
Yes,
it really dropped.
But when she was at the corner
of the General Post Office
she thought:
"Did it really drop?"
She went back to have a look.
It really dropped.
When she was again at the corner
she thought:
"Didn't I drop that letter
in front of the box?"
And she returned again
and again
up to three times.

And every time that lady
goes to mail a letter
she has to go through the same thing.
>She knows that it is nonsense,
>but she would not be able
>to go home
>without that nonsense.
>She is no longer concerned
>about the letter;
>she is concerned about something else,
>she is concerned about a ritual.
In the gospel Jesus
speaks about people
to whom something like that happened
in their religious practices.
He spoke about people
who could not eat
if they had not washed their arms
up to their elbows
before.
He spoke about people
who after coming back from the market,
could not start cooking
without sprinkling some water
over themselves
before,
people who could not use a pan or a pot
without having turned them round
in the water
seven times to the right
and seven times to the left
like an Irish nun
making some tea.
>People caught
>in their religion
>by things,
>by rituals,
>by rites
>invented
>by themselves.

People who because of those rites
overlook what religion
is really about.
> There is that mother
> who happened to be very sick
> that Sunday morning.
> She could not go to church.
> She really could not.
> But she had always been going before,
> and now she felt hopeless,
> and unsafe, and insecure
> expecting something terrible to happen
> at any moment
> because of that.
> And when just by accident
> her child then falls down the steps
> she says:
> "Of course,
> I knew
> something was bound to happen;
> you know,
> I did not go to church,
> you see!"

There is that other person
who becomes very upset
because he suddenly remembers
that he forgot
to take his Bible
with him
during his safari
as he is accustomed to do.
He almost turns green
at the thought.
> All this can grow in a person
> and Jesus said
> that in the case of the Pharisees
> it had grown to the point
> that it had completely overgrown
> their real religion,
> the service God asks from us.

And he said:
"Think of what I told you;
remember the religion
I am asking from you;
do not stick to self-imposed laws and rules
that might undo
the service asked for."
   James in his letter
   explains what that service is about.
   He writes:
   "Pure unspoiled religion
   in the eyes of God the Father
   is
   coming to the help of orphans and widows
   when they need you.
   Pure unspoiled religion is
   keeping yourself uncontaminated
   by the ways of the world,"
      being attentively interested
      in a world
      where justice,
      his justice,
      where equality,
      his equality,
      where human life,
      the life he gave,
         are respected
         and honored.

43.

HE TOOK HIS TIME

Mark 7:31–37

Jesus had definitely come
to heal all,
but he did not heal
them all
at all.
> That day he was surrounded
> by people:
> people from Tyre,
> from the Decapolis region,
> from his own country,
> and in a sense
> from the whole world.
And yet
he took that one man
who was deaf and mute
aside,
in private,
behind a bush,
alone.
He put his fingers
in his ears,
he touched his tongue
with a wet finger,
and he said:
"Ephphatha,
be opened."
> He took his time
> for that man,

while all the others
were milling around.
He took his time
to put his fingers
in his ears;
he took his time
wetting his finger;
he took his time
touching his tongue;
he took his time
speaking to him;
he took his time
asking him
not to tell anyone
what had happened.
He did not want to attract
the whole world.
He did not want to take up
that type of responsibility.
But he definitely
wanted to heal them all.
    And that is why
    he showed us
    what *we* should do
    and what *we* can do
    in the world in which
    we live:
        the world of our family,
        the world of our work,
        the world of those who depend on us,
        the world of those we meet,
        the world of those we live with,
    and if each one of us
    would take that world
    as seriously as he took
    the world in which he lived,
    all would change.
    He knew that he could not do
    it alone;

he did not want to do it
alone either.
He knew that he would only be able
to reach them all
in a community
he wants to form with
us.
When he put his fingers
in the ears of that man,
when he laid his wet finger
on the tongue of that man,
he showed us
what he expects us to do
in the world in which we live,
saying:
        "Ephphatha,
        be opened."

44.

TAKING UP HIS CROSS

Mark 8:27–35

He began to teach them,
that the Son of man
was destined to suffer
grievously.
　　　Peter,
　　　who under the influence
　　　of the miracles and the signs
　　　had already decided
　　　to follow him,
　　　did not agree.
　　　He could not agree;
　　　that was not what he was
　　　looking for.
Why had he to suffer?
Many of us might have our answer
ready:
he had to suffer,
because that is what God
had ordained
from the very beginning.
He had to suffer
because that was the price
he had to pay
for our redemption.
That is how God wanted it,
and God's ways are not human ways,
as he had said
himself.

When we speak like that,
without any further ado,
God really becomes
a very, very strange kind
of being,
a vengeful, pitiless,
bloodthirsty entity,
clamoring, so to speak,
for the blood of his son
that innocent lamb,
drop after drop
after drop.
And if that is true
it is not even so much
our sin
that killed Jesus,
but it was *because* of our sins
that he was sacrificed
by God.
Did Jesus mean
that his Father wanted his death
when he said
that he was destined
to suffer so grievously?
I wonder.
I think
that he had realized
that he would not be able
to survive his effort
to bring justice and love
into an unjust and hateful world.
He was speaking
about something
we all know.
Aren't we saying
the same thing
of the people
who want to be just
and who want to undo
corruption among us?

Let me give you a very simple
example
on how Jesus was killed
and why he was killed
and why he had to be killed.
An example even a child
might understand.
In Nazareth there was a school.
And one year Jesus
was in Standard Four.
Once the teacher
had to attend a meeting
and she appointed
the head-boy of the class
to take care of the class.
She gave him a copy-book,
and she said to him:
"If any talk while I am away
write their names in this book,"
and she left.
The head-boy took the book and
sat at the desk,
but nobody talked;
they were all very afraid.
And then that boy
got an idea.
He went to the children
in the class
and he told them,
"If you don't give me ten cents,
I am going to write
your name in my book
and you will be punished
when the teacher comes back,"
and they all paid that blackmail,
those ten cents.
Except one.
He was sitting
in the third row;

he refused
and his name was
Jesus,
son of Joseph and Mary,
and when the teacher
came back
his name was the only one
in the book
and he was punished;
he was rapped
over his knuckles
three times
and they all
laughed.
      It is that simple story
      that repeated itself
      all through his life
      at an ever more serious level.
That is why he had to die
in that world
of ours;
there was no escape
from death
for him.
      They did not forgive him
      that he refused to play their game;
      they did not forgive him
      that he did not use his power
      as they did;
      they did not forgive him
      that he was just,
      where they were unjust;
      they did not forgive him
      that notwithstanding his own
      biological urges
      he was the only one
      not exploiting the misery
      of a woman
      to relieve himself.

He died
because
THEY
killed
him.
 Brothers and sisters,
 aren't we killing him too
 when we refuse
 to introduce and respect
 justice and love
 around us?
Did you never bribe?
Did you never lie?
Did you never profit
from the weakness
of another?
 Brothers and sisters,
 did we never frustrate his kingdom,
 did we never cripple good new initiatives,
 did we never laugh at those
 who really work at a change?
It is we
who kill him,
we are
the reason
for his death
in the world
in which we live.
 Let us convert,
 let us rise
 with him
 from
 that
 death.

45.

BEING DELIVERED INTO THE HANDS OF MEN

Mark 9:30–37

Jesus said:
"I am going to be delivered
into the hands of men
and they are going
to kill me."
      A biblical saying,
      typical of Jesus,
      nice,
      solemn,
      and terrible.
      But not,
      not at all,
      applicable only
      to him!
Today
about 1,370 children
—the normal daily average—
are going to be born
in this republic of Kenya,
delivered into the hands of men.
How are they going to be received:
      with joy,
      with open arms,
      with a blessing;
      or with closed fists,

a hard mouth,
a curse;
or not at all,
thrown in a latrine pit
or in a city-council
dustbin?
Tomorrow
about two thousand new students
are going to be registered
at this University.
How are they going to be received,
        by all those administrators,
        custodians, wardens,
        professors, and others
        involved in their registration?
        Those students
        making their last arrangements
        for their trip over here
        must be wondering about that
        themselves.
        They are already old enough
        to know
        what might happen.
We all know
because we have all been
in need
of being received,
not only as a child
but so very often
in our lives,
        when we were registering
        for a school,
        when we were queueing up
        in front of the building
        with our papers
        in our hands
        and we were waiting and waiting
        and the person who should receive us
        was first having an endless phone call,

and then he reached for his newspaper,
and then someone
from behind in the queue
came to the front
and proved to be his brother,
and then he took his tea
and then, finally, he started
to attend to the queue,
but at the moment
it was your turn
he closed the door
for an hour
and you waited and waited
and when he finally
opened the door again
he looked at your papers
and said:
"You should have written your name
in block letters.
Next."
That is
how things,
not always,
but much too often
go.
That is what Jesus
was talking about
when he said
that he was going
to be delivered
into the hands of men,
into the hands of us,
and he added:
"They will kill me,
they will *not* receive me."
He came unto his own,
he came to his own home
and his own people
did not receive him.

While Jesus was worrying
about this,
while he saw their hostility,
his disciples were worrying too
and ironically
they were worrying about
the same issue,
but the other way round:
who is going to be the master
among us;
in whose hands
are the others
going to be delivered?
Who is going to be
the boss,
who is going to have
the last word,
who is going to give
the final decision,
who is going to sit behind
the desk,
who is going to attach
his signature,
who is going to receive
all those people queueing up?
Who among us
is the greatest
and the most important;
into whose hands are the crowds
to be delivered?
While Jesus complained
about the destructive powers
and the dangers
of some being masters
over others,
they were trying
to assure
that mastership
over each other,
and he said:

"Stop it,
    don't speak in terms
    of being master."
And he took a child
and he put his arms
around that child
and he whispered
to them:
    "Please,
    receive these little children,
    receive each other,
    welcome each other
        in your families,
        in your schools,
        in your jobs,
        in your work,
        in your business."
And he,
who was not going
to be received by men,
but who was going to be killed
by them,
said:
    "Anyone who welcomes
    a child,
    a newcomer,
    a human being
    in my name,
    welcomes me,
    and he who welcomes me
    welcomes my Father
    too!"
Let us think of that,
not only when we are queueing up
in front of the desk
of someone else;
let us think of that
when we are sitting
behind that desk
and others need us,

and others are delivered
into our own,
our very own hands,
because the one delivered thus
is always
Jesus
Christ.

46.

THE RUBBISH-HEAP OF THE KINGDOM

Mark 9:38-43, 47-48

Everyone seems to know
what hell is.
It is a place
with an eternal fire,
with stinking sulphurous smoke
and the grinding of teeth
all the time,
with worms that,
surviving the fire,
crawl through your flesh
and a clock
that from a wall
in all this confusion
ticks as a kind of contrast
very regularly:
     "always,"
     "never,"
     "always,"
     "never,"
     "always *in*,"
     "never *out*."
In the gospel reading of today
Jesus speaks
about hell.

When he does that
he uses a word
that you did not hear in the text
because it was translated
into English.
He uses the word
GEHENNAH,
one of the words
for the English HELL.
        And because Jesus
        used that word
        the Jews and the others
        in Jerusalem who listened
        knew exactly what he was talking
        about.
When we think
about hell
we think
about something
we never saw,
        nor smelled,
        nor heard,
        nor felt.
But when Jesus
spoke about hell
his listeners
knew what he was talking
about.
His listeners
had seen that place,
they had smelled it,
maybe they were even standing
in its smoke
while he talked.
They had seen
the eternal everlasting fire;
they had seen
the worms crawling
through that part of the place
where the fire had not yet touched.

Because GEHENNAH
was the ever-burning
rubbish-dump
of Jerusalem,
where the city-council workers
emptied
all the dustbins
of town.
And it is
in this way
that we might really
find
Jesus' message.
    You know
    what ends up in dustbins:
    food that is not eaten,
    food that is spoiled,
    wrappings and paper,
    dust and dirt,
    empty bottles
    and waste,
    the things we could not use,
    the things that broke down,
    all those things that do not function
    anymore
    and are, therefore, thrown away.
That is what Jesus
said:
"If you are not useful
in the building
of the kingdom:
human life,
the human family,
the human community,
you are going to be thrown away
by me
on the rubbish-heap of
my kingdom
called
GEHENNAH."

He does not seem to say
that you will burn there
eternally;
he does say
that the fire there
is eternal,
but he seems to suggest
that in that fire
all the useless items
are going to be burnt
to ashes.
In that way Jesus
seems to be
very near to that African idea
in which everyone tries
to destroy
and wipe out
even the memory
of an evil person
who dies,
to end his or her influence.
So,
we should be useful,
we should be a help,
we should be well-functioning cells
or organs
in his kingdom
to come,
in whatever
we do
or decide not to
do.
Amen.

47.

WHAT GOD HAS UNITED

Mark 10:2–16

To understand the gospel text of today
we should refer to the text from Genesis
read as the first reading (Gen. 2:18–24).
That Genesis text
is a very mysterious reading.
It is a mysterious reading
because it is about our beginnings.
Beginnings are difficult
to understand.
It is also a reading
that seems to explain
one of the most common questions
asked by the male students
when,
all over the world,
they are meeting
their female partners.
    A student looks at those partners
    from top to toe,
    and he asks one,
    while she is looking at him
    also from top to toe,
    "Where do you live,
    what is your hall,
    where is your room,
    what is the number?"

And she will betray
that, her secret,
only if what she sees
is according to her
worth seeing.
Why is the human urge
for a partner
so strong?
The story about the beginning
seems to give the answer:
she was made out of him;
she is looking for where
she came from,
and he is looking
for his lost rib.
That story of today
is very often used
in a strange way.
It is very often used
to indicate
that the two sexes are
unequal.
Man was created first;
woman was created as a
help to him;
the first man was not born
from a woman,
and the first woman was born
from a man;
woman is his rib;
man is original,
woman is derived;
man was God's real thought,
woman was God's after-thought;
and so on.
It was because of all this
that the readers of the Bible
really ruled over
their women.

When the woman they had married
did not please them any more
they gave her a piece of paper
to certify that fact
and they sent her
into the street.
     It is against that type
     of treatment
     that Jesus protests
     today.
They had not even read their Bibles
very well;
they read
with a very heavy bias.
     They said man is the first,
     woman is the second,
     therefore woman is less.
     They said woman is formed
     from man,
     therefore man should rule
     woman.
       But that man,
       was he not formed
       from MUD,
       and should therefore
       MUD rule over
       man?
       Did not God say in man's case:
       You are made out of the earth,
       and therefore you are more important
       and you should rule earth"?
They said that man gave woman
her name,
just as he had given names
to all the animals
to rule over them.
And in that way, they said,
the Bible clearly indicates
that he should rule over her

—and does not every woman
still lose her name
when she marries;
does not every Miss Nyambura
become a Mrs. Kamau?
But they forgot to say
that man gave that name
to woman
after the fall;
as long as things had been right
he had never done a thing like that!
Let us try
to re-read the story,
to see what is really
told.

God created a *human being*,
God put that person in this world,
surrounded by plants and animals,
covered by the sky and the clouds,
lit up by the sun and the moon and the stars,
light to be awake in,
and the dark to sleep.
He gave that human being
the whole wide world,
but that person
was alone,
utterly alone,
not only genitally
or sexually,
but in other ways too:
speechless,
helpless,
undialectical,
undynamic,
in total isolation.
And God saw
that this was no good.
God saw that this human being
could not find
an equal.

So God put that being
to sleep,
and while that person
did not notice anything,
God took that person's rib
and worked on it,
and no advice was asked for
at all
in anything,
and God made *her*
and at the same time *him*,
and then God introduced her
to him.
He did not give
her a name.
He said:
"flesh of my flesh,
bones of my bones!"
We are the same!
He found in her,
and she found in him
an equal and yet a partner,
and together
they started to live
in this world.
And now we can answer
that question we asked:
why is the human urge
for a partner
so strong?

     That urge goes deeper
     than "playing sex" genitally.
     That urge goes deeper
     than our desire to reproduce.
If that would be all,
love would be an infinite
even within the reach of dogs.
     That urge is built
     on the deepest needs
     in our personality;

it belongs to the very depth
of our being.
A man needs a woman
and a woman needs a man
to be able to survive
harmoniously
in this world,
not only for a few minutes
of pleasure,
but in a lasting relationship,
an equal partnership
in which problems
are tackled
and solved
in complementarity.
    And that is why Jesus said:
    no sending away,
    no hopping around,
    it will not solve your problems
    and you are even unfair
    to yourself.
And I think
that he might have meant
this
even in a wider context.
    The affairs in this world
    and in the church
    are too much divorced
    from women.
    There, too,
    they are sent
    away,
        and that is why
        those affairs
        are no good,
        unbalanced,
        too violent,
        onesided,
        wrong,
        and not divine.

48.

RUNNING FOR HIS LIFE

Mark 10:17–30

A man came running up to him.
He ran for his life.
He wanted to change it.
He fell on his knees before Jesus
and he asked
with big eyes:
"What should I do
to be perfect?"
> The text does not say
> that he was young,
> but all commentators
> say
> that he must have been
> very young
> because of that question:
> what should I do to be perfect?
An older man
does not ask a question
like that anymore.
Older people would like
to be perfect,
but did you ever meet an older person
who still really hopes to be perfect?
> Here at the University
> are not the *ideals* of the first year
> the *disillusions*
> of the second and the third,
> of the fourth and the fifth years?

The older people
know what it would cost
to be perfect.
They know that the price
cannot be paid
in this world of ours.
> Jesus knew that too
> and that is most probably
> why
> he did not give him
> a direct answer.
> He dodged the question.
> He questioned its validity
> in our human context.

He said:
"Why are you calling a human being
good?
No one is
good.
Why do you speak about human
perfection?
Only God is
good
and
perfect."
> And then he gave a description
> of human goodness
> in common terms:
>> do not kill,
>> do not steal,
>> do not commit adultery,
>> do not bear false witness,
>> honor your father and your mother.

But the young man
was really young;
he did not give up.
The "proposed" ideal
did not satisfy him.
And he said:

"All that
I have been doing
during all my life,
what more should I do?"
And then Jesus said:
        "You should enter the
        kingdom of God,
        but there is one thing you lack,
        and that is the fact
        that you have
        too much.
        Forget all you have acquired
        up to now.
        Give it away to the poor,
        hand it out
        and follow me."
And as you have heard
already so very often before,
at that moment the face of the young man
fell,
he walked away sad,
because he had very much.
And if we are not careful,
that young man
who walks away
out of the sight of Jesus,
departs as well
from our sight.
        That young man
        cannot teach us anything;
        he does not apply
        to our case
        anyway.
        He was different from us
        from the very beginning:
        he was rich
        and we are not.
        The lesson does not
        apply.

Didn't Jesus speak about others
when he continued
and added:
"How hard it is for those
who have riches
to enter the kingdom of God.
My children,
how hard it is,
the kingdom of God,
for those people.
It is easier for a camel
to pass through
the eye of a needle
than for a rich person
to enter that kingdom of God."
All this applies
to others,
to those with their farms,
their hotels,
their bars,
their gold,
and their elephant tusks.
It is not about us.
But did you notice
the reaction of his disciples
when he said all this?
They did not seem to reason
as we do.
They said:
"But if that is the case
who can be saved?"
Because,
they suggested,
who is not rich,
who did not acquire?
Who is not filled up with
loves,
habits,
needs,
skills,

customs,
longings,
thoughts,
desires,
dreams,
land,
children,
friends,
parents,
families,
wives,
and husbands?
All kinds of things,
all kinds of persons,
all kinds of relations
that threaten us
not to be with him
and with his kingdom
in an all-out effort
to establish here
on earth
already a foretaste
and a start
of the kingdom
to come.
   It is here
   that we DO come in.
   It is here that we find
   the reason of
   our coming together
   in order to work out
   the establishing of his kingdom,
   not of his church
      —that church is one
      of the means—
   but of his kingdom
   here among ourselves:
      in the lecture-halls,
      in the catering unit,
      in our relations,

in our sports,
in our halls of residence,
in respect for our elders,
in our help to the needy
among us,
in charity
and justice.
We should be running
for that
life.

49.

AUTHORITY AND HIS COMMUNITY

Mark 10:35–45

All around us
in this world
people are continuously
trying to get elected,
trying to get promoted,
trying to get to the top,
the very top.
It is a pushing
and a pulling
that is going on
every week,
every day,
every hour,
all the time:
>who will be first,
>who will be second,
>who will be third,
>who will be the boss.
This is not bad.
Someone should be at that top.
It is even good,
under one condition,
and that is the condition
Jesus talks about
when confronted
with James and John

263

in their drive
to the top.
    James and John
    came to Jesus;
    they had a favor
    to ask.
    Jesus asked them
    in his turn:
    "What favor?"
    And they said:
    "Would you please
    allow us
    to sit in your kingdom
    one at your right side,
    and one on your left?"
Jesus does not even
answer their question
really.
He only said:
"It is not up to me
to make a decision
like that."
But then he added:
"But why do you want
those places?
What for?"
    And not only the two of you,
    he suggested,
    but even those other ten
    who were so indignant
    that James and John
    had been asking
    for those places
    that they themselves
    had been hoping
    for.
He answered
his own question
saying:

"I know why.
I will tell you.
You want to have
power.
Power
in the old way.
You want to make
your authority
to be felt;
you want to profit
by your position.
You belong
to the old pagan world,
a world not yet influenced
by me!"
　　"In my kingdom,
　　in my community
　　it is NOT like that.
　　There those with power
　　serve;
　　they make the others
　　grow;
　　the frail ones
　　they protect;
　　they are thinking more about
　　the others
　　than about
　　themselves.
　　Look at me,
　　look at what I
　　do!"
Politicians
fighting for power
do this in order
to serve,
they say,
in order
to profit,
they hope.

But let us not
blame them.
That kind of power dynamics
does not play only
at that level.
It plays everywhere
where power is involved.
It plays also
where our power is involved.
Are we living
a pagan life,
or are we
with Christ?

50.

ALONG THE ROAD

Mark 10:46–52

He was sitting
at the side of the street.
He was blind
and he wanted to see.
He was sitting in the gutter;
everything that is not welcome
in a street
ends up in its gutter:
banana peelings,
old paper bags,
bones,
dung,
all the dirt from the houses,
and beggars.
>He had ended up there also.
>Now and then a dog
>came to sniff at him,
>a child would throw
>a stone
>and rarely,
>very rarely
>somebody would take pity
>on him.
It had been quiet
all morning,
but suddenly he heard
a growing noise
in the distance.

It came nearer
and nearer.
Was it a riot?
Did they catch a thief?
Had a prisoner escaped?
The confusion around him
grew,
and then he heard
somebody shout:
     "Alleluia"
     and
     "light of the world"
     and
     "I came to bring life"
     and
     "the crippled will walk"
     and
     "the deaf will hear"
     and
     "the blind will see."
Suddenly he understood.
The moment had arrived
he had been hoping for.
Jesus was passing,
passing *his* street.
And he shouted:
"Jesus have pity on me!"
But the others,
the seeing ones,
only interested in their own healing,
did not want this extra
competing interference.
They put him deeper down
in the gutter
and they told him:
"Shut up,"
"Keep quiet,"
but he shouted louder
and louder:
"Jesus, have pity on me!"

Jesus stopped,
he looked around,
and he said:
"Who was asking for me?"
And the circle opened up
rather unwillingly,
but it did open up
and there he was,
blind,
groping with a stick in his hand
in Jesus' direction.
They told him:
"He is asking for you,"
and he said:
"For me?"
and he jumped up,
losing his jacket
and they hustled him to Jesus.
Jesus asked:
"What do you want me to do for you?"
He said:
"Can't you see, Sir,
that I can't see?
Please, Sir,
let me see!"
Jesus said:
"All right, see!"
And he saw;
he could not believe his eyes;
he saw;
he could not believe his eyes;
he really SAW.
It must have been
a terrific experience.
There was once a case
of a British housewife,
Sheila Hock,
who for thirty long, long years
had not been able to see.
Then she was operated on.

She was in the hospital
when her bandages came off.
She had never seen before
and suddenly she saw.
She explained later:
"It was like an electric shock,
as if something hit me."
She got a plate full of food,
the first meal she SAW,
and she said:
"I thought it would be very easy to eat,
because I could now see
what I was doing.
I would aim with my fork
for a piece of tomato
and miss it."
She had to close her eyes
to be able to eat
that first time.

    She went into the street
    to go home
    and she said:
    "I looked at the pavement
    and it was moving
    and the lamp posts and the trees
    were moving so fast
    that I wanted to shout: STOP."
And she said:
"I never knew
that the world was so beautiful.
I had a picture in my mind
of what I thought my husband would look like,
because I had felt his features,
but he was a lot better looking
than I thought
and I was pleased about it."

    She sat down in a bus
    behind an older man with a bald head
    and who had a thick, red neck
    and she whispered to her husband:

"I did not know that there were people
like that,
so ugly,
going about."
Things like that
must have happened to that man
Bartimaeus,
the son of Timaeus,
at the moment
that he SAW.
Don't you remember
how in one of the gospel stories
in which another man is healed
from his blindness
his first remark is also
about trees moving around?
　　　To see suddenly
　　　must be a terrific experience.
　　　Very many,
　　　even today,
　　　who meet Jesus
　　　have that same kind of experience:
　　　they suddenly
　　　SEE,
　　　they suddenly see
　　　ALL.
　　　You know how very many
　　　who see Jesus
　　　for the first time
　　　cannot stop talking about him.
　　　In the middle of a conversation
　　　they will suddenly say:
　　　"I met him,
　　　and all at once I saw.
　　　He is my savior,
　　　my personal savior!"
Others become at that moment
so enthusiastic
that they really would like
to make others see too.

And they write pamphlets
to witness
entitled:
"How I Suddenly Saw"
and they pin them up
on the publicity walls
in university campuses
all over the world.

> They see,
> they are healed,
> they are saved,
> and that is very good
> and I wish that all of us
> would carry something of that experience
> in our hearts
> always.

But it is not all.
When the man of the story of today
was through his first enthusiasm
he picked up his stick again,
he looked around for the jacket
he had lost in his excitement,
and he started to follow Jesus
along the road,
along the road that Jesus went
to establish and to manifest
the kingdom of his Father.

> A difficult road
> leading to glory,
> but also a road that all the time
> resembles a way of the cross.
> A road full of joy,
> a road leading to final happiness,
> but a road on which he,
> that Son of God,
> *not an instrument of this world*
> *but a tool in the hands of his Father,*
> had to give himself
> from moment to moment,
> from day to day.

That blind man
followed him
along the road
the moment he saw,
and those who see as he did
because they have met Jesus
are invited to do the same.
They are invited to follow him.
And we belong
to that very crowd,
don't we?

51.

AFTER THAT NO ONE DARED ANY MORE

Mark 12:28–34

A scribe
came to Jesus,
an intellectual,
a theologian,
who had been bending
over his Bible
all his life.
> He was wearing specs
> on his nose,
> and the glasses of those specs
> were not even very clean
> because his studies
> did not leave him the time
> to clean them.
His eyes were bloodshot
from all his readings
during the day
and during the night.
> But the more
> he read,
> the less he knew,
> up to the point
> that his confusion was
> now
> almost complete.

He did not see
anything
anymore;
he did not know
what to do
any longer.
He had been reading
so many things,
he had been studying
so many questions,
he had so many answers
to those questions
that he did not even know
anymore
what the main thing
in life
should be.
    And that is why
    he came to Jesus
    with those specs
    on his nose,
    with his blurred eyes
    and his confused mind,
    and he asked:
    "Which is the first
    of all the commandments?
    What is the main
    thing?"
Jesus answered
and he said:
    "The main thing
    is
    to love God
    and to love your neighbor
    as yourself."
And suddenly
the learned scribe
saw,
he saw the light,

he saw the way out of
his confusion,
and he said:
    "Well spoken,
    thank you,
    thank you very much;
    what you say is true,
    to love God and your neighbor
    is the thing.
    It is more important
    than anything else,
    more important
    than whatever sacrifice
    we might bring.
    Thanks,
    now I know."
But Jesus
continued
and said:
    "Indeed,
    now you know,
    now you see,
    now you understand:
    you are not far
    from the kingdom of God
    because of that.
    You are standing
    on its threshold."
He stood
at the threshold
only
at the moment
that he saw.
That seeing
did not make him
enter.
His insight
did not make him
part
of the kingdom.

He had to take
a further step.
    He had to start
    loving God
    and his neighbor
    in *deed*.
The text says
that from that day onward
nobody dared
to ask
him
any question
anymore.
They did not dare,
because they knew
his answer.
    They would have
    to start to love
    God and their neighbors.
    They would have
    to love them
    as Jesus loved them.
And that was too much,
too much asked.
They preferred
to stick
to other things,
to holocausts
and sacrifices,
to spiritual exercises,
endless prayers,
and mortifications.
    To love God
    and to love the other
    as you love
    yourself?
    We prefer
    to remain
    at the threshold
    of that kingdom of God,

remaining alone,
and what can you do
alone,
without those others?
Not very
much.
Nothing
at all.

52.

HIS WIDOW COMPLEX

Mark 12:38–44

One of the reasons
that we all come together here
on Sunday mornings
with our singing,
our praying,
our drumming,
our eating,
our forgiving,
and our dancing
in this Jesus community
is,
of course,
to commemorate
and celebrate
that divine member
of our human family,
our brother
JESUS CHRIST.
> If he had not been
> the one he was and is and will be,
> we would not be here now
> either.
The story about him
today
allows us to understand something
more
of his personal psychology,
of his spiritual set up.

You know
from your own experience
how important
sometimes a story
or an example
can be
in someone's life.
A boy hears
in his youth
about another part of the world
and he swears:
"Before I die
I must see that country."
A girl hears
in her youth
a story about a heroic nurse
and she says:
"I too want to become a
nurse."
          I am standing here
          in front of you
          because my grandmother
          saved for me
          all the mission journals
          she could find
          about Africa.
Every one of you
has such a story
or such stories
that explain
your life.
          Jesus had them too.
          If we could
          trace those stories
          in his life
          we would understand
          him better
          than we
          do.

One of the stories
that must have influenced
him very much
must have been the one
we heard this morning
about that widow in
Zarephath
near Sidon (1 Kings 17:10–16).
　　　It had not rained
　　　for three and a half years;
　　　there was a terrible famine,
　　　starvation all over the place.
　　　That afternoon
　　　a widow
　　　went to collect some firewood
　　　to make her last two chapatis,*
　　　one for her son
　　　and one for herself.
　　　There was flour left
　　　only for two,
　　　and the spoonful of oil
　　　to fry them.
　　　That was all they had
　　　standing between them
　　　and death.
　　　Then Elijah comes along,
　　　the prophet who had closed
　　　the heavenly irrigation-works.
　　　He asked for some food,
　　　and she gave him
　　　all she had.
That story must have impressed
Jesus
very much
because the first time
he preaches in Nazareth
he uses her example
to explain
himself.

He must have been thinking
of her
when he was sitting
that morning
in the temple
looking at the treasury-box
in which all kinds of people
were throwing their money
from rattling
and loud clanking bags.
And then
in that row of rich people
very politely and submissively
greeted by the temple-*askaris,***
the scribes, priests, and all the others
who lived from that treasury,
there is again
that widow
with her two five-cent pieces
carefully knotted
in her handkerchief.
She stepped in front of the box
unknotting her coins;
the others were getting impatient
already,
and she dropped her
two five-cent pieces,
and was pushed on
immediately.
Jesus stood up,
his disciples too,
and he said
to their astonishment:
"Did you see
that lady?
She gave all she had,
everything;
she gave more than anyone
else."

Brothers and sisters,
he was doing that
all his days,
all his nights,
all the time:
      giving and having
      everything he had
      in view of the kingdom
      to come.
His appreciation
of those two widows
belongs to the dynamics
that made him tick
in his life.
      And if we want to be like him,
      if we want to have his blood
      and life
      in us;
      if we want to be related
      and akin
      to him;
      if our baptism
      in him
      means anything
      to us,
      then our lives too
      should integrate
      the example
      of those two widows
      who gave all they had
      in view of God,
      his kingdom
      and community
      to come.
When he took his bread
that last evening
of his life,
when he took his cup
and said:

"This is my body,
this is my blood,"
he must have been thinking
of those two,
that widow in Zarephath
and the one in the
temple.

Chapatis: pancakes of flour, water, and oil.
**Askari:* (armed) guards.

53.

HE IS VERY NEAR

Mark 13:24–32

The gospel of today
is about the end,
about distress:
>   a sun that darkens,
>   a moon that consequently dims,
>   stars that are falling,
>   powers that are shaken.
But the gospel of today
is also about a beginning:
>   a Son of men
>   who comes in power
>   and light
>   to collect
>   all his chosen ones
>   forever and ever.
It is because of these texts
that very many of us
and very often
are rather confused:
>   when will he come?
>   where will he come?
>   how will he come?
And they point
at earthquakes and tornadoes;
they point at the armament race
and the *consequent* famines;

they point
at the sins
and the crimes
and they say:
>   "He is near,
>   very near,"
although he had said:
>   "Do not point here,
>   do not point there;
>   nobody will know
>   nobody will see,
>   only the Father."
And he never came,
notwithstanding all the prophets,
up to now.
But that is not true;
he came over the last two weeks
to three of you:
>   he came to Patrick Wanjiika
>   who died of cancer;
>   he came to Elisah Omondi,
>   who fell out of a landrover;
>   he came to Pauline Mugo,
>   who overturned with a car.
When we hear texts
like the one today,
we think about another end,
we think about the end of the world
and in that way
we neutralize
the force
of those texts.
>   We should not apply
>   them to the world;
>   we should apply them
>   to ourselves,
>   not to be frightened,
>   but in order to direct our lives.

That is what Patrick Wanjiika did.
In February of this year
his leg was amputated
because of a cancer.
About ten days ago
the doctor told him
—he had asked that doctor
to be frank—
that there was no hope.
His roommate called me
to his room.
He was in his room.
I asked him:
"How old are you?"
He said:
"I hope to become twenty-one
on November the seventh."
I asked him,
"Why do you say:
I hope?"
He said:
"I am going
to die."
        He did not weep,
        he did not complain,
        he was reading the gospels.
        I said:
        "You are reading the Bible."
        He said:
        "Yes,
        he is very near.
        Can I please go for communion,
        can you hear my confession,
        can you give me the anointment
        for the sick?"
I said:
"Would you like
to get it now?"

He said:
"Oh, no,
that is not necessary,
he is not as near as that;
tomorrow morning
will do."
I asked him:
"Shall I bring him here?"
"Oh, no,"
he said,
"I will come
to him."
        And he came
        to this chapel;
        he was sitting in the pew
        over there
        preparing himself
        on his knees,
        and that was difficult
        because of his artificial leg.
I had phoned the vice-chancellor,
Professor Joseph Mungai,
about what Patrick had asked.
He had asked me:
"When will it be?"
I said:
"At 9:30."
He asked:
"How long will it
take?"
I said:
"About twenty minutes."
He came,
in time.
        Those three chairs
        were standing there
        and there we sat
        with the burning Easter candle
        and the oil,

he in the center,
the vice-chancellor to his right,
and I at his left.
He said
that he was not afraid to die,
but he said
that it was going to be
a terrible blow for his family,
who had invested all they had
in him,
and who had not been able
to let any of his brothers or sisters
continue their studies
because of him.
Saturday he went home,
and five days later
he died.
Jesus had been very near
indeed.
Brother and sister,
I don't tell you this
to frighten you
or myself.
Jesus did not tell
the story about his nearness
to frighten us,
but to help us
to live our lives
in a wise way:
not to clutter it
with useless items,
not to use it
on things that never will last,
but on life that will last
forever and ever.
This world
will pass;
all things
will pass;

but human life
will never pass.
Let us
think of
that
while making
our
choice.

54.

OUR LORD JESUS CHRIST, UNIVERSAL KING

John 18:33–37

We Christians
are quite ready
to admit
that Jesus Christ
is king.
    It gives us
    a sense of belonging,
    of trust, confidence,
    and even security.
We hang a cross
around our necks,
a medal or a rosary;
we put his picture
on the wall,
he with his bleeding heart,
or we enthrone
his statue
on a cupboard
in our room.
    He is our king,
    and when you walk
    through so many streets
    that is what you see
    in shops
    all through Nairobi.

It is not always Christ,
it could be Krishna,
the Aga Khan,
it could be Guru Nanak
or another saint.
In Christian shops
it is
Jesus.

> There he hangs on the wall
> with his great large eyes
> looking at what is going on:
> no wonder that his eyes
> are almost always
> very sad,
> because what he sees
> is not his kingdom
> at all.

We are quite ready
to admit
that he is king.
We are even willing to admit
that he should rule
our inner hearts,
but that he should rule
human life
we do not admit
at all.

> Think of the bombs,
> think of the wars,
> think of the dying children,
> think of this world.
> Yet human life
> is what his kingdom is.
> That is where he should
> have his reign.
> His kingdom should relate
> to all we do
> at this University
> and in our lives:

arts or architecture,
medicine or science,
commerce or law,
veterinary medicine or agriculture,
engineering or education,
planning or journalism.
It is that human life
he is the head
and the king of.
His kingship
does not depend
only on him.
Don't overlook
that beautiful piece
of dialogue
between Pilate and him.
Pilate
asked him:
"Are you king?"
Jesus
did not give
an answer.
He could not.
Whether he is
a real king
or not
does not depend
solely on him;
it depends on
us,
and that is why
he later says to Pilate:
"It is you
who say it,
yes, king
I am."
If we say:
"He is king,"
he is and will be.

If we don't say it
nor mean it,
he is not.
    But,
    brothers and sisters,
    he should be,
    because he really
    is the only answer
    in the wilderness
    of this world
    and this our human life.
    Isn't he?
    He is.
    Amen, amen,
    alleluia.

INDEX OF SCRIPTURAL TEXTS